Workshop on Information Extraction and Entity Analytics on Social Media Data

Held at the 24th International Conference on Computational Linguistics (COLING 2012)

Mumbai, India
9 December 2012

Editors:

Sriram Raghavan
Ganesh Ramakrishnan

ISBN: 978-1-62748-355-1

Printed from e-media with permission by:

Curran Associates, Inc.
57 Morehouse Lane
Red Hook, NY 12571

proceedings.com

Some format issues inherent in the e-media version may also appear in this print version.

Printed by Curran Associates, Inc. (2013)

Association for Computational Linguistics
209 N. Eighth Street
Stroudsburg, Pennsylvania 18360

Phone: 1-570-476-8006
Fax: 1-570-476-0860

acl@aclweb.org

Additional copies of this publication are available from:

Curran Associates, Inc.
57 Morehouse Lane
Red Hook, NY 12571 USA
Phone: 845-758-0400
Fax: 845-758-2634
Email: curran@proceedings.com
Web: www.proceedings.com

Preface

The growth of online social media represents a fundamental shift in the generation, consumption, and sharing of digital information online. Social media data comes in many forms: from blogs (Blogger, LiveJournal) and micro-blogs (Twitter) to social networking (Facebook, LinkedIn, Google+), wikis, social bookmarking (Delicious), reviews (Yelp), media sharing (Youtube, Flickr), and many others. The information inherent in these online conversations is a veritable gold mine with the ability to influence every aspect of a modern enterprise – from marketing and brand management to product design and customer support. However, the task of drawing concrete, relevant, trustworthy, and actionable insights from the ever increasing volumes of social data presents a significant challenge to current day information management and business intelligence systems. As a result, there is growing interest and activity in the academic and industrial research communities towards various fundamental questions in this space:

- How do we collect, curate, and cleanse massive amounts of social media data?
- What new analytic techniques, models, and algorithms are required to deal with the unique characteristics of social media data?
- How does one combine information extracted from textual content with the structural information in the "network" (linking, sharing, friending, etc.)?
- What kind of platforms and infrastructure components are required to support all of these analytic activities at scale?

Currently, relevant work in this area is distributed across the individual conferences and workshops organized by different computer science research disciplines such as information retrieval, database systems, NLP, and machine learning. Furthermore, a lot of interesting innovations and hands-on experience from industrial practitioners is not publicly available. This workshop aims to bring together industrial and academic practitioners with a focus on an aspect of this problem of particular relevance to COLING – namely, robust and scalable techniques for information extraction and entity analytics on social media data.

We have put together an interesting program which consists of keynotes from two well known researchers, Marius Pasca (Google Research, Mountainview) and Dan Roth (University of Illinois at Urbana Champaign) which provides both an industry and academic perspective to the challenges of information extraction from social media data.

Marius Pasca's talk is on *Extracting Knowledge from the Invisible Social Graph*. The background, needs and interests of Web users influence the social relations they choose to have with other users, and the knowledge exchanged among users as part of those relations. The same factors influence the choice of queries submitted by users to Web search engines. Multiple users may refer to entities and relations of general interest in their posts and updates shared with others, just as they may refer to them in their search queries. In his talk, Marius discusses the types and uses of knowledge that can be extracted from collectively-submitted search queries, relative to extracting knowledge encoded in social media data.

Dan Roth's talk is on *Constraints Driven Information Extraction and Trustworthiness*. Computational approaches to problems in Natural Language Understanding and Information Extraction often involve assigning values to sets of interdependent variables. Examples of tasks of interest include semantic role labeling (analyzing natural language text at the level of "who did what to whom, when and where"), information extraction (identifying events, entities and relations), and textual entailment (determining whether one utterance is a likely consequence of another). However, while information extraction aims at telling us what a document says, we are also interested in knowing whether we can believe the claims made and the sources making them.Over the last few years, one of the most successful approaches to studying global decision problems in Natural Language Processing and Information Extraction involves Constrained Conditional Models (CCMs), an Integer Learning Programming formulation that augments probabilistic models with declarative constraints as a way to support such decisions. In this talk, Dan will present research within this framework, discussing old and new results pertaining to training these global models, inference issues, and the interaction between learning and inference. Most importantly, he will discuss extending these models to deal also with the information trustworthiness problem: which information sources we can trust and which assertions we can believe.

Tien Thanh Vu et. al. present an interesting application of predicting the stock prices by extracting and predicting the sentiments present in Twitter messages of these stocks. This is a very practical application of anticipating the fluctuations of stock markets using information gleaned from social media

Finding trends in social media is a very important activity and has a lot of practical applications, that include marketing. Nigel Dewdney et. al., present a study of the trends originating from blogs and contrasts it with trends from news on current affairs. Does information present in blogs reflect mainstream news or does it provide other trending topics which is significantly different from news: this is the matter of study in this work.

Twitter, a microblogging service, has been a very rich source of social media content and contain a large amount of short messages. Due to the short nature of messages, this type of an information extraction task can be quite challenging. The work by Kamel Nebhi discusses a rule-based system for identifying and disambiguating named-entities from tweets. Apoorv Agarwal et. al. present a system to perform end-to-end sentiment analysis of tweets. The system also explores the design challenges in building a sentiment analysis engine for twitter streams.

Organizing Team
Workshop on Information Extraction and Entity Analytics - 2012

Workshop chairs:
Sriram Raghavan and Ganesh Ramakrishnan

Diamond sponsors

Tata Consultancy Services
Linguistic Data Consortium for Indian Languages (LDC-IL)

Gold Sponsors

Microsoft Research
Beijing Baidu Netcon Science Technology Co. Ltd.

Silver sponsors

IBM, India Private Limited
Crimson Interactive Pvt. Ltd.
Yahoo
Easy Transcription & Software Pvt. Ltd.

Organizing Committee:

Sriram Raghavan (IBM Research - India)
Ganesh Ramakrishnan (IIT Bombay)
Ajay Nagesh (IIT Bombay)

Programme Committee:

Sunita Sarawagi (IIT Bombay)
Indrajit Bhattacharyya (Indian Institute of Science, Bangalore)
Rajasekar Krishnamurthy (IBM Research - Almaden)
L. V. Subramanian (IBM Research - India)
Sundararajan Sellamanickam (Yahoo! Labs, Bangalore)
Rahul Gupta (Google Inc, USA)
Anhai Doan (University of Wisconsin-Madison and WalmartLabs)
Kevin Chen-Chuan Chang (University of Illinois at Urbana-Champaign)
Parag Singla (IIT Delhi)
Mausam (University of Washington at Seattle)

Invited Speakers:

Marius Pasca (Google Research)
Dan Roth (University of Illinois at Urbana-Champaign)

Table of Contents

Workshop on Information Extraction and Entity Analytics on Social Media Data

Program

Saturday, 9 December 2012

09:15–09:30	Welcome and Introduction
09:30–10:30	**Keynote Talk** *Extracting Knowledge from the Invisible Social Graph* Marius Pasca, Google Research
	Paper presentations – Session 1
10:30–11:00	*Named Entity Trends Originating from Social Media* Nigel Dewdney
11:00–11:30	*Ontology-Based Information Extraction from Twitter* Kamel Nebhi
11:30–12:00	Tea break
12:00–13:00	**Keynote Talk:** *Constraints Driven Information Extraction and Trustworthiness* Dan Roth, University of Illinois at Urbana-Champaign
13:00–13:30	– *Buffer* –
13:30–14:30	Lunch
	Paper Presentations – Session 2
14:30–15:00	*An Experiment in Integrating Sentiment Features for Tech Stock Prediction in Twitter* Tien Thanh Vu, Shu Chang, Quang Thuy Ha and Nigel Collier
15:00–15:30	*End-to-End Sentiment Analysis of Twitter Data* Apoorv Agarwal and Jasneet Sabharwal
15:30–16:00	*Leveraging Latent Concepts for Retrieving Relevant Ads For Short Text* Ankit Patil, Kushal Dave and Vasudeva Varma
16:00–16:15	Closing Remarks

Named Entity Trends Originating from Social Media

Nigel Dewdney
Department of Computer Science
University of Sheffield
acp08njd@sheffield.ac.uk

ABSTRACT
There have been many studies on finding what people are interested in at any time through analysing trends in language use in documents as they are published on the web. Few, however have sought to consider material containing subject matter that originates in social media. The work reported here attempts to distinguish such material by filtering out features that trend primarily in news media. Trends in daily occurrences of nouns and named entities are examined using the ICWSM 2009 corpus of blogs and news articles. A significant number of trends are found to originate in social media and that named entities are more prevalent in them than nouns. Taking features that trend in later news stories as a indication of a topic of wider interest, named entities are shown to be more likely indicators although the strongest trends are seen in nouns.

KEYWORDS: Social media, Trend analysis.

Proceedings of the Workshop on Information Extraction and Entity Analytics on Social Media Data, pages 1–6,
COLING 2012, Mumbai, December 2012.

1 Introduction

The detecting and tracking of popular topics of discussion through trend analysis has become a keenly studied an developed area with the rise in use of social media. Various algorithms have been proposed for finding the ”hot topics” of current interest in user communities with various social media providers, such as Twitter.com, providing a trending topics service. Typical topics that are keenly discussed are often around breaking and current news stories. Occasionally the social media may be the first to break the news, as famously with the Haitian earthquake of 2008, or even be at the centre of news stories such as with the events of the ”Arab Spring”. However, sometimes stories and information may originate from social media, rapidly spreading and rising in popularity. Such instances of the spread of information have been described as ”going viral”. The question arises, then, as to what information may lie in social media that might have sufficient potential to be interesting to many others, but is largely lost due to the dominance of current affairs. Are social media topics of interest, other than what is in the news, general in nature or are they about specific things?

Although much of the news available online is sourced from and published by professional media organisations, there are an increasing number of people using web logs, or “blogs” where authors provide original material and opinions on topics of interest to them [18]. Micro-blogs, as popularised by Twitter, provide a more immediate shorter form, but being shorter are less likely to be a rich source of information at the individual message level. Alvanaki et al. [2] have likened tweets (twitter postings) to chat, the longer blogs form being more akin to publication of articles. The study here, therefore, will focus on personal blogs.

Many trending topics have been found to related to current news stories, however Lloyd et al. have found that a small percentage of these originate from personal blogs [21]. In such cases it may be that the popularity of the topic itself becomes the story, as an example of interest “going viral”. A news story of this type, it could be argued, would be a report of the kind of phenomenon of interest here, i.e. a trend originating in social media.

Rising popular activity in social media may not be isolated to national and international situations involving a large population. Speculation around and interest in imminent or recent product releases for example is one area where information may be more readily found in social media than in the main stream. Such information is of interest to marketing companies; social media is an important source for product feedback and marketing strategy monitoring.

A recent example is that of interest surrounding an upcoming release of a computer game called "Black Mesa", a fan remake of "Half Life", a popular commercial PC game from the previous decade. The game has been the subject of much discussion amongst enthusiasts which increased following the announcement of a release date. Discussion even got as far as a news report on the BBC news website on the $3rd$ September 2012. The Graph in Figure 1 shows the number of blog posts published each day during a three week period up to the BBC news story, as measured with Google’s blog search engine.

A natural question to ask, then, is what is the nature of trending topics that *originate* in social media, i.e. those not sparked by topics already in the news? Are there characteristics in trending features that show social media originated trends to be significantly different from news stories, or do we see the citizen journalist [6] in action? The work described here begins to investigate these questions.

As topics that originate in social media are of particular interest here, it will be necessary to

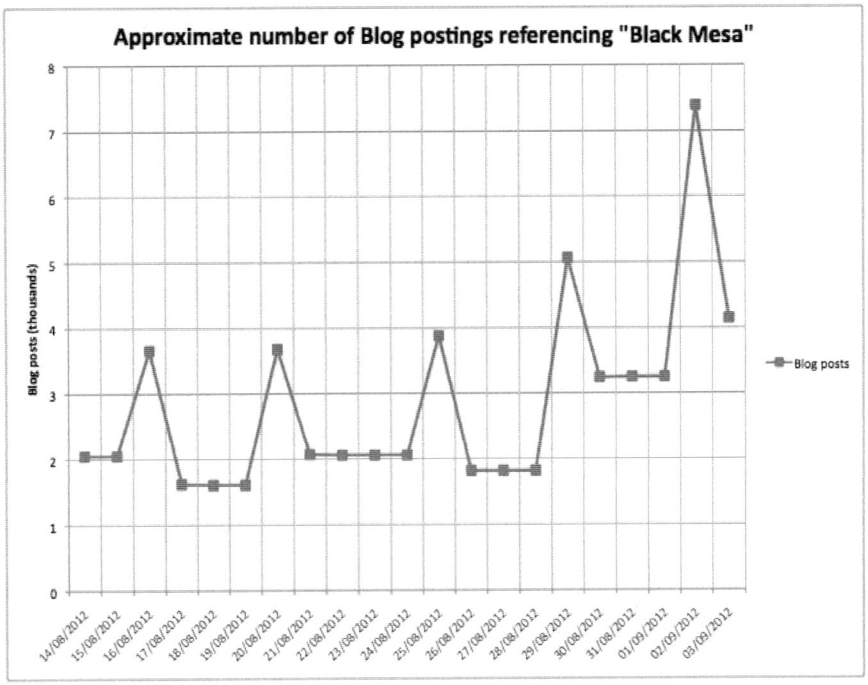

Figure 1: Blog post results for daily search for "Black Mesa game" using Google's blog search engine

identify those that originate in reports made by the mainstream media so that they may be distinguished from those originating in social media. Some of these topics may go on to be of interest in mainstream news, while we would expect many to remain within the "blogosphere". As an initial step towards characterising trending topics with social media origins, we examine the nature of the trending features: Are specific entities or generic nouns more prevalent, and what are the relative strengths of their trends?

This paper reports on an analysis of trending common nouns and named entities originating in social media, i.e. after having filtered mainstream news stories out, using the ICWSM 2009 Spinn3r dataset [7]. The rest of the paper is organised as follows: section 2 summarises recent relevant and related work; section 3 provides a description of the data and the method of analysis employed; section 4 describes the analysis of the results; finally section 5 gives conclusions and outlines future work.

2 Related work

Trend analysis has been a popular area of study in recent years with the rise in popularity of social media as a means to disseminate information, provide opinion and facilitate discussion. Discovering what the popular topics within populations are at any particular time is of potential interest to many, including politicians, journalists, and marketing departments. Numerous approaches have been suggested and implemented. Detection of changes in language use as new documents are published is often at the heart of these methods, as new topics emerge and are written about.

A burst in activity may be expected with sudden popular interest in a topic, and reflected in document features. Various different models have been proposed for modelling streams of text to account for bursts. Church found that words that show a high likelihood of re-occurring in a document under a Poisson model, one would often consider to be a "content" word [10]. Sarkar et al. used a double Poisson Bayesian mixture model for term "burstiness", to determine such "content" words [26]. Baroni and Evert have taken a different approach for document term burst modelling [5], proposing the use of document frequency rather than term frequency.

Many approaches to detecting new emerging topics have been based on detecting bursts in term use. For example, Kleinberg examined time gaps between term occurrences in email data and found bursts in email topics seemed to coincide with interest to the author [17], and Kumar et al. observed bursts in links being established in the evolution of the "Blogosphere" [18]; Franco and Kawai have investigated two approaches to detecting emerging news in blogs [13], through blogosphere topic propagation measured by evolution of link numbers, and by blog post clustering; Viet-Ha-Thuc et al. used a log-likelihood estimate of an event within a topic model [16]; and Glance et al. have examined bursts in phrases, mentions of people, and hyperlinks in blogs given a background of blogs published in the preceding two weeks [15].

Other approaches to topic detection and tracking have sought to include structure, see [23], [11] for examples; and topic classification as in [30], or [14], where Gabrilovich et al. used bursts of articles with high divergence from established topic clusters to detect new stories. However new topic detection is difficult though as noted by Allan et al. [1], who comparing the task to that of information filtering, show new story detection in tracking is poor.

Micro-blogs, such as that facilitated by Twitter, have provided a rich source of data for those studying trends and their evolution. Micro-blogs, or "Tweets", are restricted to 140 characters, and has been likened to chat rather than publication by Alvanaki et al. [2]. In their "En Blogue" system, they detect emerging topics by considering frequent tags and co-incident tags (these are augmented by extracted named entities). Twitter provides its own proprietary trending topics service, but others have sought to provide similar functionality. Petrović et al. have investigated first story detection in Twitter micro-blog feeds [24]; Mathioudakis and Koudas describe a system that detects and groups bursting keywords [22]; Cataldi et al. consider a term to be emerging if it frequently occurs in the interval being considered whilst relatively infrequently in a defined prior period, generating emerging topics from co-occurrence vectors for the considered interval [8].

Research has also looked at how trends evolve through social media and how content spreads: Cha et al. have studied how media content is propagates through connected blogs [9]; Simmons et al. have examined how quoted text changes as it is communicated through social media networks [27]; and Lerman and Ghosh have studied the spread of news through the Digg and Twitter social networks [19]. Asur et al. have examined how trends persist and decay through social media [3] finding that the majority of trends follow news stories in Twitter, with re-tweeted items linked to news media providers such as CNN and Reuters.

Trending topics not linked to stories reported in the mainstream media have been found. Lloyd et al. found a small percentage of blog topics trended before the news-stories were published [21]. They compared the most popular named entities in news and blogs on a mentions-per-day basis finding that maximal spikes could be present in one medium before the other. Leskovec et al. in investigating concept of "memes", short phrases, and how they evolved in news websites and blog publication, found a small percentage of quotations to originate in personal blogs rather than news reports [20]. This small percentage of material indicated by these two studies is makes up the source of interest here.

3 Data and analytic approach

Blog data for this study comes from the ICWSM 2009 corpus, made available to researchers by the organisers of the 3rd International AAAI Conference on Weblogs and Social Media (2009) [7]. The dataset, provided by Spinn3r.com, comprises some 44 million blog posts and news stories made between August 1st and October 1st, 2008. For the experiments reported here the data is pre-processed. Blog posts that have been classified either as "MAINSTREAM NEWS" or "WEBLOG" are extracted, while "CLASSIFIED" postings and empty postings (here less than 3 characters long) are discarded. Applying trend analysis to each class will allow the likely trend source to be identified.

Many trend analysis approaches analyse simple lexical features, before using other techniques, such as clustering and feature co-occurrence analysis, to improve the semantic richness. (See [22], [8], [2] for examples.) Trending topics involve tangible (named) entities; Azzam et al. suggested that a document be about something – its topic – and that something would revolve about a central entity [4]. There is also evidence that names can be effective in information retrieval tasks [28], and searching for names has been shown to be useful concept in news archive search [25].

Rather than relying solely on lexical statistics to determine both content bearing features and trends, the approach taken applies part-of-speech tagging and named entity recognition prior to statistical analysis. The Stanford CoreNLP toolset, using the supplied 4-class model for English text without any modification [29][12] is used here. The training data used for the model was that supplied for CoNLL 2003 and is made up of Reuters Newswire. Although the training data does not perfectly match blog data, articles of interest may be expected to have some similarity in style, i.e. "reporting". It is assumed that the performance of the natural language processing is sufficiently robust such that output will be substantially correct English given noisy input. (Note: Input data is pre-processed to remove any html mark-up for this investigation.)

We consider a trending topic to be one that shows an increase in the number of occurrences of associated features, be they nouns or named entities, from that expected. For this we employ a a traditional Poisson model parameterised by the observed mean feature occurrence rate. The model assumes that features occur at random and independently, the intervals between occurrences being Poisson distributed. The reciprocal of the expected interval gives the expected frequency. Positive deviations (decrease in arrival time) from expectation are indicative of a trending feature, with strength measured by the size of the deviation.

A random variable X with a Poisson distribution, expectation $E[X] = \lambda$, has the model:

$$P(X = k|\lambda) = \frac{\lambda^k e^{-\lambda}}{k!}, k \geq 0 \qquad (1)$$

The mean frequency is simply the inverse of the expected gap between occurrences for the feature k, i.e. $1/\lambda$. As the variance of the Poisson distribution is also λ trend strength can be measured as the number of standard deviations, $\sqrt{\lambda}$, the gap reduction is from the mean. It follows that for feature k with expected frequency $\frac{1}{\lambda_k}$ and observed frequency $\frac{1}{\lambda'_k}$, the strength of a trend in k is given by:

$$T(k) = \frac{\lambda_k - \lambda'_k}{\sqrt{\lambda_k}} \tag{2}$$

A daily trend in feature occurrence is measured in standard deviations given by $T(k)$ from the expected frequency, calculated by averaging observed frequency over preceding days. Feature frequencies are calculated on a daily basis with average frequencies being calculated accumulatively. A number of days of observation are required to establish a reasonable estimate of the average frequency $1/\lambda_X$ for each feature $X = 1, 2, \ldots$ In this study, one week of observations are used prior to application of trend detection.

Following the method of Lloyd et al. [21],trend analysis is applied independently to the "MAINSTREAM NEWS" and "BLOG" classes of posts in the corpus, thus allowing the likely trend source to be identified. The focus, then, is on named entities and nouns that show trending behaviour, originating in social media blogs.

4 Experiments and Results

Over the two full months of data in the corpus, August and September 2008, there are 1,593,868 posts from mainstream news sources, while there are 36,740,061 blog postings. Of these, 1,428,482 news stories and 27,074,356 blogs contain at least one entity, and all bar 157 blog postings contain English nouns (although there is no guarantee the post is actually in English).

The amount of material produced each day is not consistent however as can be seen from the graphs shown in figures 2 and 3, although News postings show a periodic nature as one might expect. There is a notable increase in noun output in blogs but not in news towards the end of the period, although this increase is not seen named entity output. The number of postings made per day shows no significant change suggesting that the rise in noun output is due to a relatively small number of long blog postings that do not mention a correspondingly higher number of named entities.

We now turn our attention to those features that demonstrated a rising trend in occurrence in blogs during the period of the corpus, either exclusively or prior to a trend in news articles. Minimum criteria for feature selection are that they have a minimum of over five occurrences or show a positive deviation of over five standard deviations from their average daily occurrence at the time of their maximum positive trend. Trends for features that have trended in news articles within the previous seven days are not considered. No trend analysis is carried out for the first seven days to allow a fair estimate of average daily occurrence to be established, so occurrences on the 8th August are the first to be considered, being reported therefore on the 9th. This selection process yields a total of 47639 features that show a positive trend originating in social media from the 8th Augusts 2008 to 30th September 2008. An average of 60.4% of these trending features are also seen in later trends within news articles. The break-down across nouns and named entities is given in table 1.

A high proportion of nouns that show trending behaviour originating in blogs, about 73%, are within the vocabulary of news articles. The lack of editorial control together with tagger inaccuracies account for much of the remainder. A much lower proportion of named entities that originally trend within blogs are also seen in news at all. We may conclude that while some people, organisations, and places etc. may be of topical interest in the social media, only

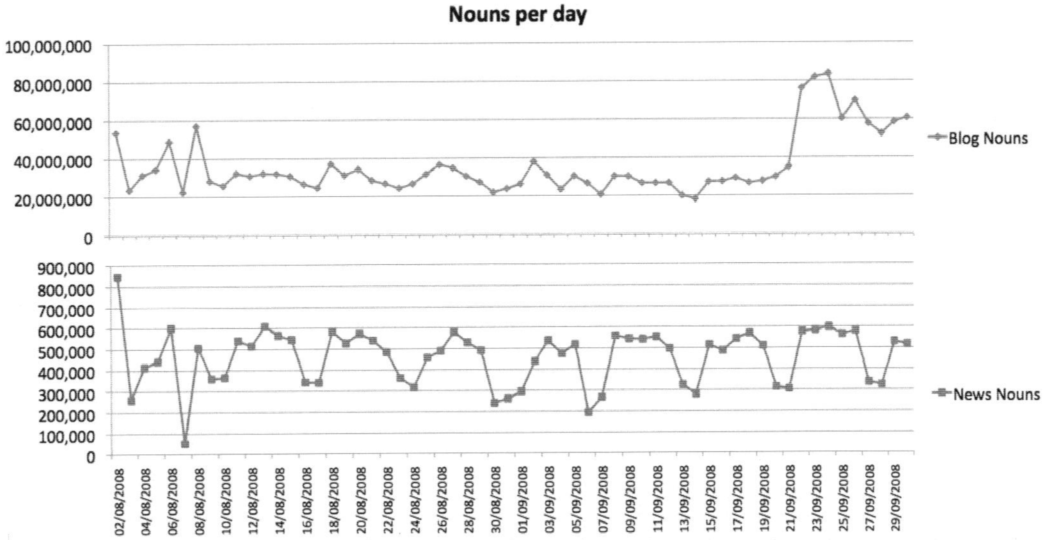

Figure 2: Nouns in blogs and news per day in ICWSM 2009 corpus

Type	No. Trending	No. in News pre/post trend	%
Nouns	12157	8827	72.6%
Misc	11260	5303	47.1%
Location	9809	5331	54.3%
Person	9365	5993	64.0%
Organisation	9823	5889	60.0%
Totals	47639	28776	60.4%

Table 1: Unique social media originating trending feature totals & amount in news use

abut half of them (between 47% and 64%) are also in the sphere of interest of the mainstream media organisations.

As trend strength is measured relative to the average occurrence of a feature rather than in absolute occurrence numbers, the most popular nouns and entities are not necessarily the same as those that show the strongest trend. Table 2 notes the top ten most frequent nouns and the top ten strongest trending nouns with their average frequency and trend strengths at the time of they showed their strongest trend. There are two observations to make: Firstly that a significant number of these "nouns" are not correctly identified by the part-of-speech identifier and named entity tagger, being either broken mark-up or proper nouns; Secondly the strongest trending contain the unidentified proper nouns.

Tables 3,4,5 and 6 show the top ten by average occurrence and by maximum trend strength for Organisation, Person, Location and Miscellaneous names. The most frequent entities are mentioned several thousand times a day (about an order of magnitude less than the most frequent nouns). Their trend strengths range from a few 10's of std deviations from their average daily occurrence to a few thousand, similar in strength to the top occurring nouns. The trend strengths are typically well under those shown by the top ten entities by maximum trend strength, which are in the region of several thousand standard deviations. These too are an order of magnitude less than trend strengths shown by the maximally trending nouns. Overall,

Top Occurring			Top Trending		
Noun	Avg per Day	Max Trend	Noun	Avg per Day	Max Trend
QUE	67072.4	958.9	WON	184.2	92152.5
%	60444.3	1002.7	– – – – – – – – – – ...–	14.8	83949.8
THINGS	52755.2	410.4	3A	36.1	76574.3
COM	51408.7	5322.4	BEHAR	59.4	75912.3
SOMETHING	48963.0	547.2	PEARCE	87.6	69001.3
DA	46427.7	4269.0	PROP	163.2	68665.7
GIRL	44684.9	1255.9	<BR?/>	810.1	51689.2
MUSIC	44454.6	740.1	PIVEN	705.3	50291.6
DVD	44327.5	4001.1	ANTOFAGASTA	16.2	48510.5
EL	41919.9	666.7	JEUDI	142.1	46578.9

Table 2: Top ten 'nouns' by average daily occurrence and by trend strength in blogs

Top Occurring			Top Trending		
Noun	Avg per Day	Max Trend	Noun	Avg per Day	Max Trend
GOOGLE	10443.0	303.9	ILWU	0.8	5929.3
APPLE	3138.6	577.7	ADM	24.4	5459.2
UA	3083.5	2359.9	OHIO STATE	211.1	5452.2
YAHOO	2279.1	2409.3	STATE FARM	15.4	5147.4
VMWARE	2142.2	1494.6	SOA	243.7	4935.9
HOUSE	2009.3	146.9	IBM	1944.4	4341.8
IDF	1945.2	1663.6	HEALTH MINISTRY	52.9	4122.3
IBM	1944.4	4341.8	BUCS	82.4	4000.3
MCKINSEY	1726.6	1059.5	ACORN	109.3	3967.0
HET	1641.5	1610.4	USAF	115.4	3965.7

Table 3: Top ten Organisations by average daily occurrence and by trend strength in blogs

Top Occurring			Top Trending		
Noun	Avg per Day	Max Trend	Noun	Avg per Day	Max Trend
OBAMA	34008.6	64.1	BEHAR	16.4	7119.4
MCCAIN	14677.7	53.3	KWAME KILPATRICK	517.2	6698.0
JOHN MCCAIN	12280.5	68.7	ALICE COOPER	63.2	6345.6
JACK	5415.7	3098.2	FREEMAN	111.9	6155.8
JESUS	3924.7	1994.1	CORSI	166.0	5619.6
JENSEN	2661.4	1675.2	MRS. CLINTON	71.3	5575.4
RYAN	2163.1	2375.9	OLMERT	134.1	5238.0
DAVID	2156.5	1503.5	SANTANA	72.1	5127.6
PETER	1703.3	2613.4	BUFFETT	93.4	5101.8
GOD	1688.5	2767.8	CARL ICAHN	37.0	5028.9

Table 4: Top ten Persons by average daily occurrence and by trend strength in blogs

Top Occurring			Top Trending		
Noun	Avg per Day	Max Trend	Noun	Avg per Day	Max Trend
NEW YORK	6267.8	67.2	GOLD COAST	10.6	4005.6
INDIA	6188.3	70.4	BISHKEK	103.6	3912.0
UK	4146.9	293.8	LIMA	358.6	3683.3
FRANCE	3269.7	56.4	WELLS	18.6	3674.3
FLORIDA	3207.1	69.3	WIRED.COM	91.3	3632.4
DELHI	3171.2	1805.5	HAMPTON	30.4	3630.7
IRAN	2755.7	269.6	CALCUTTA	54.8	3613.2
ISRAEL	2750.3	371.8	HULU	167.2	3491.8
LOS ANGELES	2320.7	74.1	YUNNAN	64.9	3463.6
PARIS	2110.3	183.4	TRIPOLI	180.4	3421.1

Table 5: Top ten Locations by average daily occurrence and by trend strength in blogs

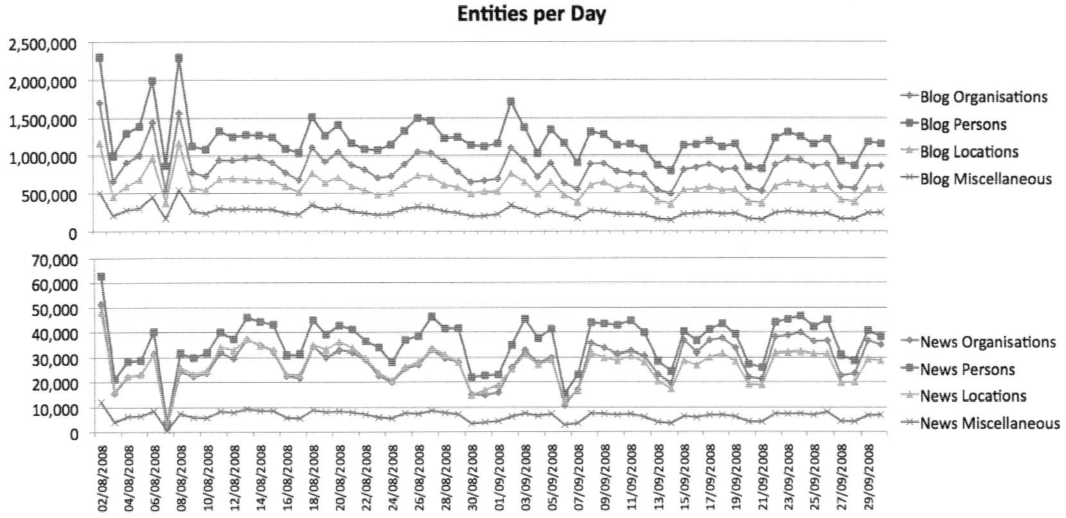

Figure 3: Entities in blogs and news per day in ICWSM 2009 corpus

Top Occurring			Top Trending		
Noun	Avg per Day	Max Trend	Noun	Avg per Day	Max Trend
INTERNET	6428.6	85.4	ALPS	42.8	2523.1
WINDOWS	1882.7	1416.4	GENESIS	76.9	2430.3
DEMOCRAT	1669.7	78.0	LITTLE LEAGUE WORLD SERIES	49.4	2263.7
GMT	1479.2	1183.7	SUMMER OLYMPIC	11.0	2050.8
ALS	1267.9	865.3	TEAM	21.3	2029.0
FACEBOOK	1217.0	1385.2	VIETNAM WAR	76.5	1928.7
TWITTER	791.6	1029.4	BOLIVARIAN ALTERNATIVE	3.9	1927.5
CHRISTMAS	786.4	1174.1	BRITONS	71.9	1772.3
JAVA	745.7	923.8	SERIE A	18.3	1765.6
MUSLIMS	703.2	665.0	CHINA OPEN	62.6	1696.2

Table 6: Top ten Miscellaneous by average daily occurrence and by trend strength in blogs

people tend to appear in trends more strongly than organisations and places, as well as showing higher average daily occurrences.

To get a sense of any linkage between average daily occurrence and maximum trends strengths in social media originated trends, the two can be plotted against one another. Distributions can be further divided into those features that are unique to language seen in social media, that which is also seen in news articles and those that also trend in news articles after a trend is seen originating from blogs. Plots for nouns and each entity type are shown in Figure 4. Also shown are the mean and standard deviation of the distributions in log occurrences and log maximum trend strength.

Trending features that are unique to blogs tend to be fewer and weaker than those that also appear in news vocabulary, although the separation is greatest for nouns. However, the presence of these for nouns at all may be for the reasons of noise and tagger errors described above. Many trending named entities occurring uniquely in blogs have average daily occurrence of less than ten per day.

Features that show trends in news after the original trend in social media tend to be the most

	Unique		Blog trending		Subsequent News trend	
	Log Occurences		Log Occurences		Log Occurences	
	Mean	Std Dev	Mean	Std Dev	Mean	Std Dev
Nouns	0.6976	0.8714	1.7296	0.7543	2.8397	0.6804
Misc	-0.2744	0.9127	0.3864	0.7157	1.4419	0.7532
Locations	-0.1258	0.9134	0.4861	0.7241	1.5045	0.8019
Persons	0.0159	0.8519	0.7401	0.8558	1.7236	0.6577
Organisation	0.0118	0.8254	0.6590	0.7933	1.6546	0.6888
	Log Max Dev		Log Max Dev		Log Max Dev	
	Mean	Std Dev	Mean	Std Dev	Mean	Std Dev
Nouns	3.3728	0.2587	3.9692	0.1692	3.8430	0.4191
Misc	2.4378	0.2214	2.5897	0.2414	2.9137	0.2129
Locations	2.5991	0.2104	2.7958	0.2299	3.0807	0.2757
Persons	2.7170	0.2390	2.9716	0.2125	3.3035	0.1868
Organisation	2.6515	0.2465	2.9165	0.2141	3.2103	0.1797

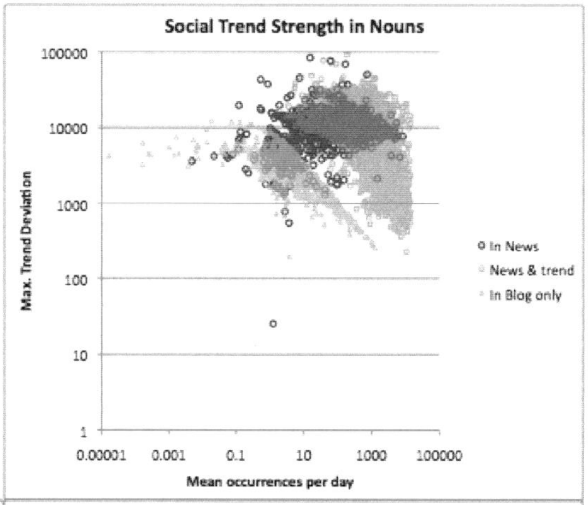

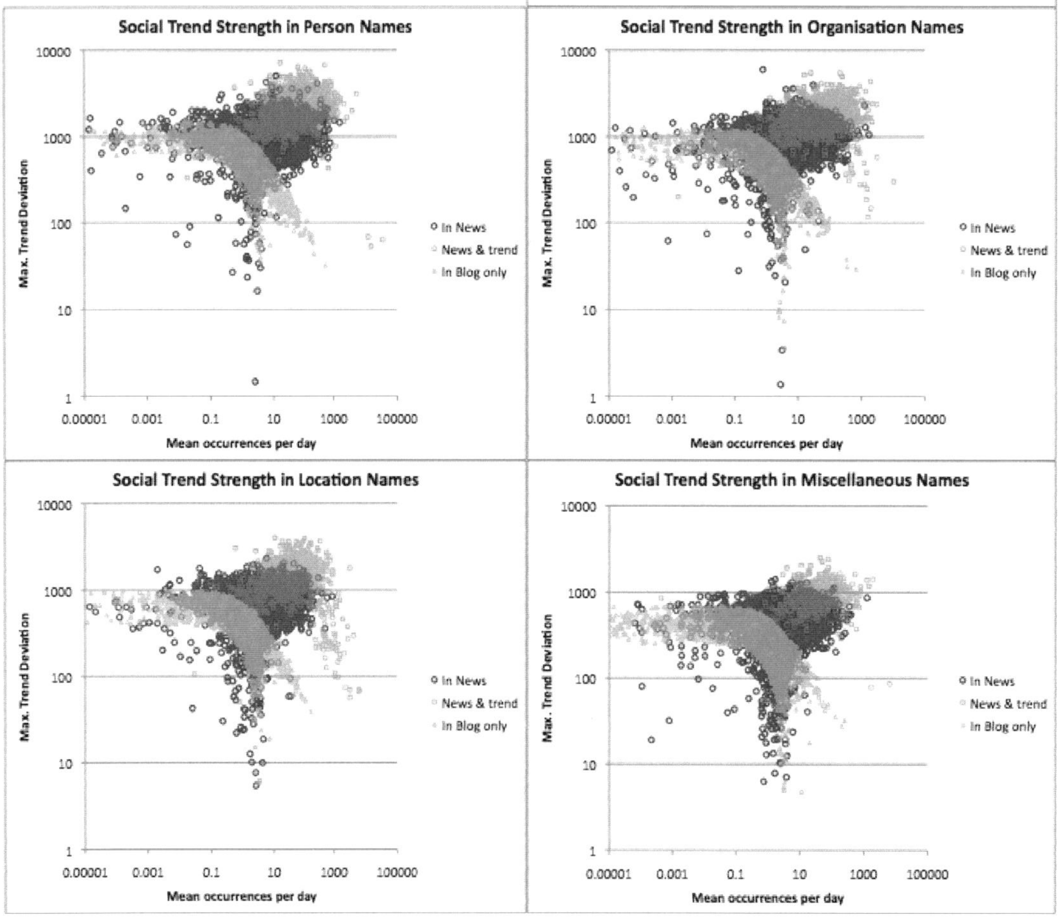

Figure 4: Distributions of occurrence per day and trend strengths for trends originating in blogs

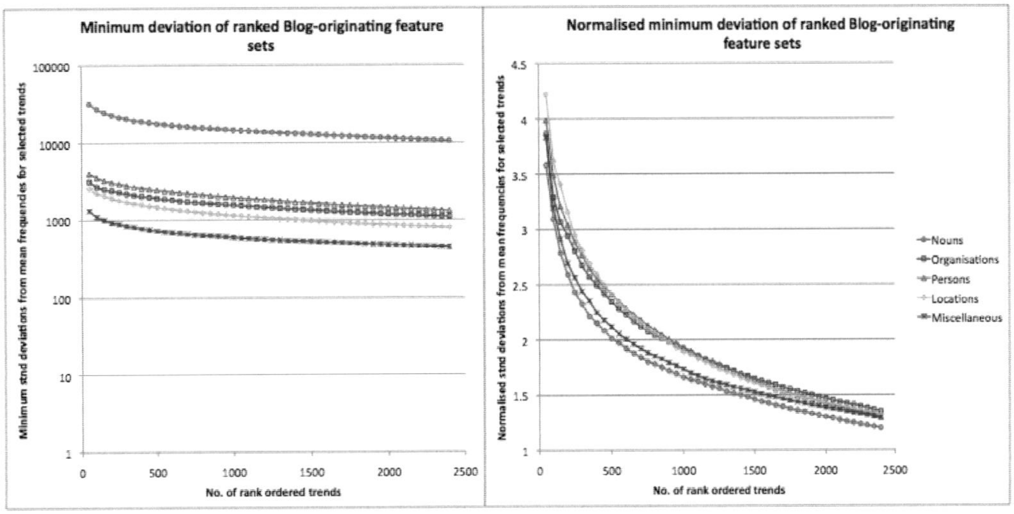

Figure 5: (a) Minimum trend strength of top n trending features (b) Minimum of top n ranked normalised trend strengths

frequently occurring. Within these features, entities also tend to show higher trend strengths and, while some nouns show higher trend strengths, nouns overall have a similar spread in trend strength as those not trending subsequently in the news: A separation in distributions of trend strength for features later trending in news and those not, is not present. Overall these distributions have significant overlap with those of corresponding feature types appearing in news articles without subsequent trends therein. The vast majority of those features showing subsequent trends in news articles have an average occurrence of at least one mention per day at the time of the trend.

These distributions suggest that entities being written about by bloggers that may be of wider interest at any particular time, tend to show trend strengths of a few hundred standard deviations from their average daily occurrence, although this can be less for very common entities (those with daily occurrence in excess of 1,000). Strengths for nouns in topics of potential wider interest tend to be an order of magnitude higher (average daily occurrence also being about an order of magnitude higher). However, this magnitude difference in trend strength is also true for nouns not subsequently trending in news articles. This suggests that comparisons between feature types would be better made having normalised by the average trend strength within a feature type.

A comparison of maximum trend strengths in feature types given the top *n* trending features is shown in Figure 5: Graph (a) shows the raw trend strengths while Graph (b) shows the normalised trend strengths. Note that normalisation of trend strength by feature type average de-emphasises the dominance of nouns, while the relative difference between entity types shows little change, although Locations have slightly more prominence.

In a monitoring application, it is likely one would wish to select only the most significant trending features. This suggests applying a threshold to observed trend strength. Graph (a) in Figure 6 shows the number of features that would be selected from this corpus given a normalised feature trend strength threshold. Each feature type is plotted separately as well as

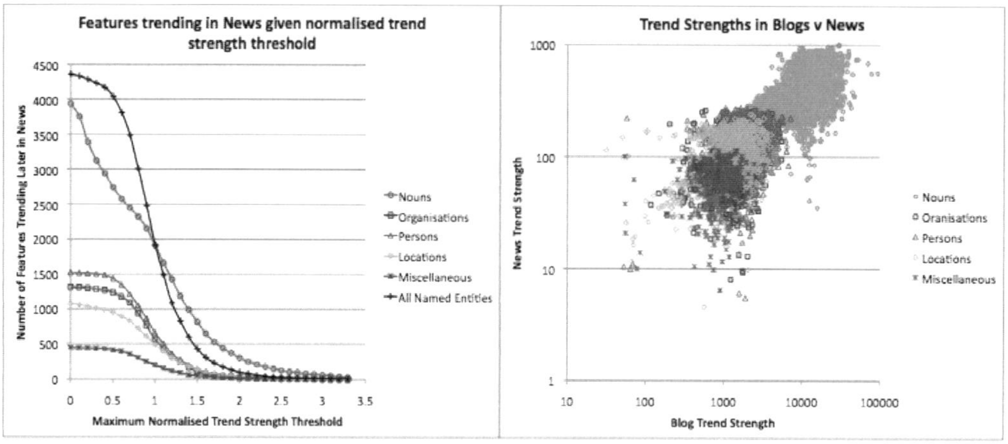

Figure 6: (a) Number of features selected for given normalised trend strength threshold (b) Relative trend strengths for those seen first in blogs and subsequently in news

for combined named entities. Note here that although the total number of trending entities outnumbers that for nouns, the spread of entity trend strengths has a narrower spread that for them. Figure 6 Graph (b) shows the un-normalised trend strength for features that also show a later trend in mainstream news articles, against that subsequent news trend strength. This shows that there is some correlation between the strength shown in the news trend and that shown in the original social media trend. If trending in news stories is indicative of wider interest then this suggests that trending features originating in social media are quite likely to be of topical appeal. Furthermore, as we have seen, many of these features are likely to be named entities.

5 Conclusions

This initial study into the type of language in trends originating in social media has shown that although much that is discussed by bloggers is whatever is currently topical in mainstream media, there is a significant amount of material of wider interest that originates in blogs. Furthermore it suggests that a significant proportion of this material may be linked to that which is later topical in news articles. The amount of material produced by bloggers is approximately 20 times greater in number of articles than professional news organisations, and the amount of individual nouns and named entities suggest their postings are also longer. Size of vocabulary is also much greater amongst social bloggers than within the mainstream media (although some of this one would consider to be erroneous or "noisy" text). There is great potential, then, for finding material in social media that is of wider interest.

Although maximum trend strengths shown for nouns are considerably greater than those shown in named entities, named entities are marginally more frequent in social media originated trends. Higher trend strengths are displayed by those features that are seen, and particularly later trend, in news articles, although these strengths are relative to the distribution seen for the feature type. Nouns trends that will later trend in news articles are not separable by trend strength alone. Selecting trends purely by highest trend strength is unlikely to be be optimal, therefore, as many trending entities of potential interest may be missed. A better strategy for selecting trends likely to be indicative of topics of wider interest would be to select the strongest trends within classes of nouns and named entities, and possibly applying appropriate thresholds. Normalisation of trend strength by average class type trend strength may be another possibility, as this seems to make trend scores for feature types more comparable. Normalised trend scores show a narrower distribution around the mean score for entities that subsequently trend in news stories than nouns, suggesting that a threshold could be effectively applied in deciding what should be considered a genuinely trending feature.

If we believe that news stories have a wide interest, then these results suggest it is more likely that the trending feature in social media is a named entity than a noun. (Even though the very strongest trend strengths seem to be displayed by nouns.) The identification and analysis of named entities as separate features to detect trends in is, therefore, potentially of great benefit when seeking to find emerging topics of interest. The Named Entity Recogniser was not trained or tuned for social media, but rather well prepared newswire text. One would expect errors to occur both in recognition of named entities and in mis-typing of detected entities, and some errors were observed. However, a sufficiently high accuracy for differences in trends to be detected was observed. The extent to which named entity detection and recognition performance may impact remains to be determined.

Given that there are a significant number of trends originating from social media, it is natural to ask whether one can predict which will go one to be subjects in the news, and what the delay between social media interest and mainstream media interest is. Further work may also focus on determining the topic(s) named entities are involved in. These are areas for future study.

References

[1] J. Allan, V. Lavrenko, and H. Jin. First story detection in tdt is hard. In *CIKM '00: Proceedings of the ninth international conference on Information and knowledge management*, pages 374–381, New York, NY, USA, 2000. ACM.

[2] F. Alvanaki, M. Sebastian, K. Ramamritham, and G. Weikum. Enblogue: emergent topic detection in web 2.0 streams. In *Proceedings of the 2011 international conference on Management of data*, SIGMOD '11, pages 1271–1274, New York, NY, USA, 2011. ACM.

[3] S. Asur, B. A. Huberman, G. Szabó, and C. Wang. Trends in social media : Persistence and decay. *CoRR*, abs/1102.1402, 2011.

[4] S. Azzam, K. Humphreys, and R. Gaizauskas. Using coreference chains for text summarization. In *CorefApp '99: Proceedings of the Workshop on Coreference and its Applications*, pages 77–84, Morristown, NJ, USA, 1999. Association for Computational Linguistics.

[5] M. Baroni and S. Evert. Words and echoes: Assessing and mitigating the non-randomness problem in word frequency distribution modeling. In *Proceedings of the 45th Annual Meeting of the Association of Computational Linguistics*, pages 904–911, Prague, Czech Republic, June 2007. Association for Computational Linguistics.

[6] S. Bowman and C. Willis. We media: How audiences are sharing the future of news and information. Technical report, The Media Center at the American Press Institute, 2003.

[7] K. Burton, A. Java, and I. Soboroff. The ICWSM 2009 Spinn3r Dataset. In *Third Annual Conference on Weblogs and Social Media (ICWSM 2009)*, San Jose, CA, May 2009. AAAI. http://icwsm.org/2009/data/.

[8] M. Cataldi, L. Di Caro, and C. Schifanella. Emerging topic detection on twitter based on temporal and social terms evaluation. In *Proceedings of the Tenth International Workshop on Multimedia Data Mining*, MDMKDD '10, pages 4:1–4:10, New York, NY, USA, 2010. ACM.

[9] M. Cha, J. Antonio, N. Pérez, and H. Haddadi. Flash floods and ripples: The spread of media content through the blogosphere. In *ICWSM 2009: Proceedings of the 3rd AAAI International Conference on Weblogs and Social Media*. AAAI, 2009.

[10] K. W. Church. Empirical estimates of adaptation: the chance of two noriegas is closer to p/2 than p2. In *Proceedings of the 18th conference on Computational linguistics*, pages 180–186, Morristown, NJ, USA, 2000. Association for Computational Linguistics.

[11] A. Feng and J. Allan. Finding and linking incidents in news. In *CIKM '07: Proceedings of the sixteenth ACM conference on Conference on information and knowledge management*, pages 821–830, New York, NY, USA, 2007. ACM.

[12] J. R. Finkel, T. Grenager, and C. Manning. Incorporating non-local information into information extraction systems by gibbs sampling. In *Proceedings of the 43rd Annual Meeting on Association for Computational Linguistics*, ACL '05, pages 363–370, Stroudsburg, PA, USA, 2005. Association for Computational Linguistics.

[13] L. Franco and H. Kawai. News detection in the blogosphere: Two approaches based on structure and content analysis. 2010.

[14] E. Gabrilovich, S. Dumais, and E. Horvitz. Newsjunkie: providing personalized newsfeeds via analysis of information novelty. In *WWW '04: Proceedings of the 13th international conference on World Wide Web*, pages 482–490, New York, NY, USA, 2004. ACM.

[15] N. S. Glance, M. Hurst, and T. Tomokiyo. Blogpulse: Automated trend discovery for weblogs. In *WWW 2004 Workshop on the Weblogging Ecosystem: Aggregation, Analysis and Dynamics*. ACM, 2004.

[16] V. Ha-Thuc and P. Srinivasan. Topic models and a revisit of text-related applications. In *PIKM '08: Proceeding of the 2nd PhD workshop on Information and knowledge management*, pages 25–32, New York, NY, USA, 2008. ACM.

[17] J. Kleinberg. Bursty and hierarchical structure in streams. *Data Min. Knowl. Discov.*, 7(4):373–397, 2003.

[18] R. Kumar, J. Novak, P. Raghavan, and A. Tomkins. On the bursty evolution of blogspace. In *Proceedings of the 12th international conference on World Wide Web*, pages 568–576, New York, NY, USA, 2003. ACM.

[19] K. Lerman and R. Ghosh. Information contagion: An empirical study of the spread of news on digg and twitter social networks, 2010.

[20] J. Leskovec, L. Backstrom, and J. Kleinberg. Meme-tracking and the dynamics of the news cycle. In *KDD '09: Proceedings of the 15th ACM SIGKDD international conference on Knowledge discovery and data mining*, pages 497–506, New York, NY, USA, 2009. ACM.

[21] L. Lloyd, P. Kaulgud, and S. Skiena. Newspapers vs. blogs: Who gets the scoop. In *AAAI spring symposium on Computational Approaches to Analyzing Weblogs*, pages 117–124, 2006.

[22] M. Mathioudakis and N. Koudas. Twittermonitor: trend detection over the twitter stream. In *Proceedings of the 2010 international conference on Management of data*, SIGMOD '10, pages 1155–1158, New York, NY, USA, 2010. ACM.

[23] R. Nallapati, A. Feng, F. Peng, and J. Allan. Event threading within news topics. In *CIKM '04: Proceedings of the thirteenth ACM international conference on Information and knowledge management*, pages 446–453, New York, NY, USA, 2004. ACM.

[24] S. Petrović, M. Osborne, and V. Lavrenko. Streaming first story detection with application to twitter. In *Human Language Technologies: The 2010 Annual Conference of the North American Chapter of the Association for Computational Linguistics*, pages 181–189, Los Angeles, California, June 2010. Association for Computational Linguistics.

[25] H. Saggion, E. Barker, R. Gaizauskas, and J. Foster. Integrating nlp tools to support information access to news archives. In *Proceedings of the 5th International conference on Recent Advances in Natural Language Processing (RANLP)*, 2005.

[26] A. Sarkar, P. H. Garthwaite, and A. De Roeck. A bayesian mixture model for term re-occurrence and burstiness. In *CONLL '05: Proceedings of the Ninth Conference on Computational Natural Language Learning*, pages 48–55, Morristown, NJ, USA, 2005. Association for Computational Linguistics.

[27] M. Simmons, L. Adamic, and E. Adar. Memes online: Extracted, subtracted, injected, and recollected. In *Proceedings of the Fifth International AAAI Conference on Weblogs and Social Media*, 2011.

[28] P. Thompson and C. Dozier. Name searching and information retrieval. In *In Proceedings of Second Conference on Empirical Methods in Natural Language Processing*, pages 134–140, 1997.

[29] K. Toutanova, D. Klein, C. D. Manning, and Y. Singer. Feature-rich part-of-speech tagging with a cyclic dependency network. In *Proceedings of the 2003 Conference of the North American Chapter of the Association for Computational Linguistics on Human Language Technology - Volume 1*, NAACL '03, pages 173–180, Stroudsburg, PA, USA, 2003. Association for Computational Linguistics.

[30] Y. Yang, J. Zhang, J. Carbonell, and C. Jin. Topic-conditioned novelty detection. In *KDD '02: Proceedings of the eighth ACM SIGKDD international conference on Knowledge discovery and data mining*, pages 688–693, New York, NY, USA, 2002. ACM.

Ontology-Based Information Extraction from Twitter

Kamel Nebhi
LATL, Department of linguistics
University of Geneva, Switzerland
kamel.nebhi@unige.ch

ABSTRACT
The popular microblogging service Twitter provides a vast amount of short messages that contains interesting information for Information Extraction tasks. This paper presents a rule-based system for the recognition and semantic disambiguation of named entities in tweets. As our experimental results shows, performance of this approach measured through BDM looks promising when using Linked Data as Freebase and syntactical context for disambiguation.

KEYWORDS: Ontology-based Information Extraction, Disambiguation, Twitter, Linked Data.

1 Introduction

Twitter is a microblogging service that plays an increasingly important role as a social network and a news media. Twitter allows users to post 140-characters messages and follow users of the world. In February 2012, Twitter had approximately 200 millions active registered users that send 175 millions tweets each day[1]. The growing popularity of Twitter is producing a vast amount of short messages (tweets) that contains interesting information for NLP tasks like Information Extraction (IE).

In this paper, we present an Ontology-based Information Extraction (OBIE) system for Twitter messages using a rule-based approach. Our system combines Named Entity Recognition (NER) and a disambiguation module. We show that our system can improve disambiguation efficiency using syntactical context and knowledge base like Freebase.

The paper is divided as follows. First we present our approach in Section 2. Then, we present the experimental setup for testing in Section 3. Finally, we summarize the paper.

2 Approach

2.1 OBIE

Information Extraction is a key NLP technology to introduce complementary information and knowledge into a document. The term "Ontology-based Information Extraction" has been conceived only a few years ago and has recently emerged as a subfield of IE. OBIE is different from traditional IE because it finds type of extracted entity by linking it to its semantic description in the formal ontology. The task of OBIE has received a specific attention in the last few years with many publications that describe systems.

For (Wimalasuriya and Dou, 2010), the key characteristics of OBIE systems are:

- *Process natural language text documents*: the inputs of OBIE systems are limited to unstructured or semi-structured documents.

[1] http://www.creativethinkingproject.com/wp-content/uploads/2012/03/CTP_SocialMediaStatistic.pdf

Proceedings of the Workshop on Information Extraction and Entity Analytics on Social Media Data, pages 7–12,
COLING 2012, Mumbai, December 2012.

- *Information Extraction process guided by an ontology*: the information extraction process is guided by the ontology to extract things such as classes, properties and instances.
- *Present the output using ontologies*: OBIE systems must use an ontology to represent the output.

2.2 Architecture

Our OBIE system is built on GATE (Cunningham et al., 2011) to annotate entities in tweets and relate them to the DBpedia ontology[2] where appropriate. The DBpedia ontology is a shallow, cross-domain ontology, which has been manually created based on the Wikipedia projects. The ontology organizes the knowledge according to a hierarchy of 320 classes and 1650 different properties.

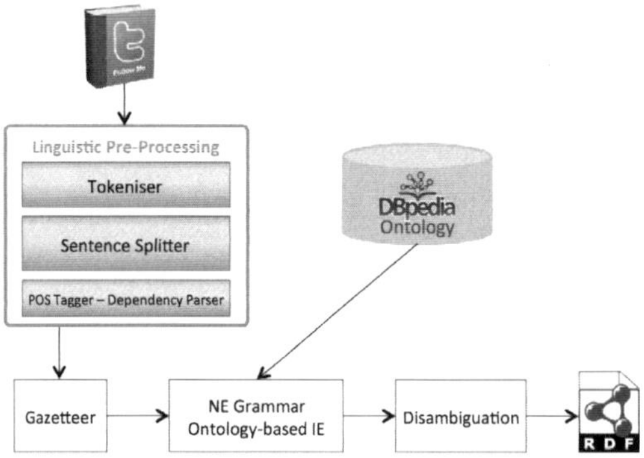

Figure 1: Ontology-based Information Extraction Architecture

Figure 1 describes the architecture of our OBIE system. The source data is a set of short messages from *BBC News*, *New York Times* and *The Times* Twitter accounts. Semantic annotation is performed by GATE with respect to the DBpedia ontology. The GATE application consists of a set of processing resources executed in a pipeline over a corpus of documents. The pipeline consists of 5 parts:

- Linguistic pre-processing
- Gazetteer (used to identify entities directly via look-up)
- Rule-based semantic annotation
- Disambiguation
- Final output creation

The linguistic pre-processing phase contains GATE components such as tokenisation and sentence splitter. It also contains specific tools like Stanford Parser for English part-of-speech tagging and dependency parsing. The gazetteer lookup phase comprises combination of default gazetteer lists from ANNIE[3] and some newly gazetteer lists extract from Wikipedia and DBpedia. The grammar rules for creating semantic annotation are written in a language called JAPE, which is a finite state transducer. The rules are based on pattern-matching using several information taken from the gazetteer and the Stanford Parser results.

[2] `http://wiki.dbpedia.org/Ontology`

[3] GATE is distributed with an IE system called ANNIE (A Nearly-New IE system). It comprises a set of core processing like tokeniser, sentence splitter, POS tagger, Gazetteers, JAPE transducer, etc.

2.3 Disambiguation process

Disambiguation process consists in determining which sense of a word is used when it appears in a particular context. For example, the string "Washington" is used to refer to more than 90 different named entities in DBpedia database. Our approach use popularity score and syntax-based similarity to disambiguate each surface form (Hoffart et al., 2011).
Popularity Score: This score is provided by Freebase API (Bollacker et al., 2008) [4]. Popularity score of entities can be seen as a probabilistic estimation based on Wikipedia frequencies in link anchor. The search Freebase API allows access to Freebase data given a text query. A large number of filter constraints are supported to better aim the search at the entities being looked for.
For example, this GET request `https://www.googleapis.com/freebase/v1/search?query=Washington&filter=(any%20type:/people/person)&indent=true` only matched persons named "Washington".
Syntax-based Similarity: After selecting candidate entities for each surface form with Freebase, our system uses the context around the surface forms. For this, we construct a context from all words in the short messages using syntactic information based on dependency trees (Thater et al., 2010). We created rules to determine the immediate syntactic context in which an entity mention occurs.
Table 1 shows examples of NER for a BBC News tweet. For this short message, the system use popularity score to disambiguate entities.

Tweet	@BBCBreaking: Hamas says senior military figure Ahmed al-Jabari killed in Israeli airstrike in Gaza.
Extracted Mentions	Hamas, Ahmed Jabari, Gaza
Candidate Entities	{Hamas, Hamas of Iraq}, {Ahmed Jabari, Abdullah Muhammed Abdel Aziz}, {Gaza, Gaza strip, Palestinian territories}

Table 1: Example of Extraction for a BBC News Tweet

3 Evaluation

3.1 The "Balanced Distance Metric"

Traditional IE systems are evaluated using Precision, Recall and F-Measure. These measures are inadequate when dealing with ontologies. In (Maynard et al., 2008), Maynard analyzed several metrics and proved that the Balanced Distance Metric (BDM) is useful to measure performance of OBIE systems taking into account ontological similarity. In fact, BDM is a real number between 0 and 1 depending on several features like:

- The length of the shortest path connecting the two concepts
- The depth of the two concepts in the ontology
- Size and density of the ontology

[4]Freebase is a collaborative knowledge base used to structure general human knowledge. It contains structured data of almost 23 million entities.

The BDM itself is not sufficient to evaluate our system, so we decide to combine the traditional Precision and Recall with the BDM measure to obtain an Augmented Precision (AP) and an Augmented Recall (AR) as follows :

$$AP = \frac{BDM}{n + Spurious^5} \quad and \quad AR = \frac{BDM}{n + Missing^6}$$

In order to demonstrate the usefulness of this measure, Table 2 presents some examples of entities misclassified by the system. All the concepts involved in Table 2 are illustrated in Figure 2, which presents a part of the DBpedia ontology.
In the first example, the predicted label `PopulatedPlace` is 2 concepts away from the key label `City` but its BDM_F_1 value is lower than the corresponding value in the fourth example, mainly because the concept `PopulatedPlace` occupies a higher position in the DBpedia ontology than the concept `BodyOfWater`. BDM also considers the concept densities around the key concept and the response concept. We can show the difference by comparing the second and the third example. They have the same predicted label `Company`, and their key labels `MediaCompany` and `RecordLabel` are two sub-concepts of `Organisation`. However, their BDM values are different. This is because the concept `MediaCompany` has one child node but the concept `RecordLabel` has no child node.

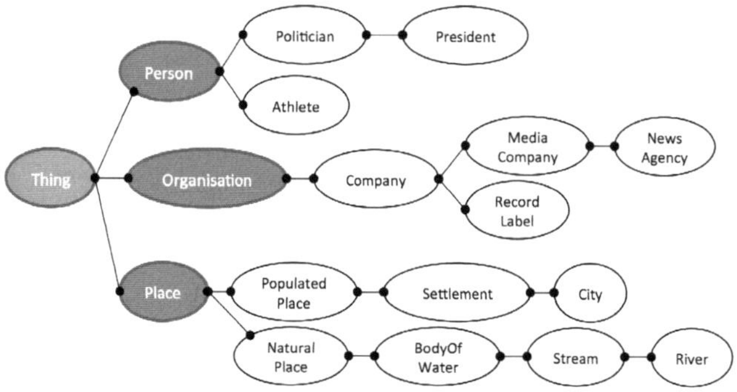

Figure 2: View of the DBpedia Ontology

Entity	Result	Key	BDM_F_1
Boston	PopPlace	City	0.43
Vivendi	Company	MediaCompany	0.55
UMG	Company	RecordLabel	0.45
Ourcq	BodyOfWater	River	0.45

Table 2: Examples of entities misclassified by the system

[5]The application marked an entity that is not annotated in the key (=False Positive).
[6]The entity is annotated in the key but the application failed to mark it (=False Negative).

3.2 Experiment

To evaluate the performance of the system we applied the processing resources on the evaluation corpora of 115 short messages from *BBC News, New York Times* and *The Times* Twitter accounts. We manually annotated these documents with the concepts of the DBpedia ontology. Then, we compare the system with the gold standard.
For the evaluation, we only use Person, Organization and Location named entity categories. In table 3, the system without disambiguation achieved a traditional F-Measure of 65% and an augmented F-Measure of 69%. Adding the disambiguation layer improve extraction effectiveness, traditional F-Measure rises to 86% and augmented F-Measure rises to 90%.

	F_1	BDM_F_1
OBIE (no disambiguation)	0.65	0.69
OBIE (with disambiguation)	0.86	0.90

Table 3: Results

Conclusion and perspectives

In this paper we introduced an approach for Ontology-based Information Extraction from Twitter. Our system provides an integrated disambiguation module based on popularity score and syntax-based similarity. As our evaluation shows, the system performed significantly better using disambiguation process.
In future work, we plan to incorporate more knowledge from Linked Data and we'll integrate the application into a ReSTful Web service.

References

Bollacker, K., Evans, C., Paritosh, P., Sturge, T., and Taylor, J. (2008). Freebase: a collaboratively created graph database for structuring human knowledge. In *Proceedings of the 2008 ACM SIGMOD international conference on Management of data*, New York, USA. ACM.

Cunningham, H., Maynard, D., Bontcheva, K., Tablan, V., Aswani, N., Roberts, I., Gorrell, G., Funk, A., Roberts, A., Damljanovic, D., Heitz, T., Greenwood, M. A., Saggion, H., Petrak, J., Li, Y., and Peters, W. (2011). *Text Processing with GATE (Version 6).*

Hoffart, J., Yosef, M. A., Bordino, I., Fürstenau, H., Pinkal, M., Spaniol, M., Taneva, B., Thater, S., and Weikum, G. (2011). Robust disambiguation of named entities in text. In *EMNLP*, pages 782–792.

Maynard, D., Peters, W., and Li, Y. (2008). Evaluating evaluation metrics for ontology-based applications: Infinite reflection. In *LREC*.

Thater, S., Fürstenau, H., and Pinkal, M. (2010). Contextualizing semantic representations using syntactically enriched vector models. In *Proceedings of the 48th Annual Meeting of the Association for Computational Linguistics*, ACL '10, pages 948–957, Stroudsburg, PA, USA.

Wimalasuriya, D. C. and Dou, D. (2010). Ontology-based information extraction: An introduction and a survey of current approaches. *J. Information Science*, 36(3):306–323.

An Experiment in Integrating Sentiment Features for Tech Stock Prediction in Twitter

Tien Thanh Vu[1,3] *Shu Chang*[2,3] *Quang Thuy Ha*[1] *Nigel Collier*[3]

(1) University of Engineering and Technology, Vietnam National University Hanoi, 144 Xuanthuy street, Caugiay district, Hanoi, Vietnam

(2) University of Bristol, Senate House, Tyndall Avenue, Bristol BS8 1TH, UK

(3) National Institute of Informatics, National Center of Sciences Building 2-1-2 Hitotusbashi, Chiyoda-ku, Tokyo 101-8430, Japan

`tienthanh_dhcn@coltech.vnu.vn`, `shuchang0011@gmail.com`, `thuyhq@vnu.edu.vn`, `collier@nii.ac.jp`

ABSTRACT

Economic analysis indicates a relationship between consumer sentiment and stock price movements. In this study we harness features from Twitter messages to capture public mood related to four Tech companies for predicting the daily up and down price movements of these companies' NASDAQ stocks. We propose a novel model combining features namely positive and negative sentiment, consumer confidence in the product with respect to 'bullish' or 'bearish' lexicon and three previous stock market movement days. The features are employed in a Decision Tree classifier using cross-fold validation to yield accuracies of 82.93%,80.49%, 75.61% and 75.00% in predicting the daily up and down changes of Apple (AAPL), Google (GOOG), Microsoft (MSFT) and Amazon (AMZN) stocks respectively in a 41 market day sample.

KEYWORDS: Stock market prediction, Named entity recognition (NER), Twitter, Sentiment analysis.

Proceedings of the Workshop on Information Extraction and Entity Analytics on Social Media Data, pages 13–28, COLING 2012, Mumbai, December 2012.

1 Introduction

Recent research into social media has looked at the application of microblogs for predicting the daily rise and fall in stock prices. In many ways microblogs are an ideal early warning about company price movements as they are freely available, rapidly updated and provide spontaneous glimpses into the opinions and sentiments of consumers about their future purchasing behaviors. Previous work such as (Bar-Haim et al., 2011) has assumed that messages containing explicit buy or sell signals about stocks are the most informative for stock price prediction although such messages typically comprise only a fraction of the available information about company sentiment. In this work we approach the task from another perspective, one in which Twitter users' sentiment, related to the company, influences the next day's market price movement. This allows us to tap into a much wider base of mood about the company's future prospects. With the high level of number of Tweets related to tech companies, we focus on predicting stock market movement of four famous tech companies namely Apple, Google, Microsoft and Amazon.

Our approach departs from another major work into sentiment analysis for tracking the Dow Jones Industrial Average (DJIA) by (Bollen et al., 2011b) in that we do not pre-assign a sentiment lexicon or assume mood dimensions. Instead we induce the lexicon automatically by association with "bullish" (a positive price outlook) and "bearish"(a negative price outlook) anchor words on the Web. Further, our work predicts stock market at company level which is deeper than whole stock market level in (Bollen et al., 2011b).

Our work seeks to contribute on several fronts: we explore the underlying relationship between sentiment about the company and stock price movements - helping to avoid the problem of identifying expert stock price pickers (Bar-Haim et al., 2011); we automatically discover sentiment bearing words that have high correlation to the stock market domain; and finally we build a named entity recognition system on Twitter data to identify and remove noise Tweets.Through a series of experiments we show the contribution of sentiment, named entities and changes in the stock market indices on a companies' future share price movement.

Although this was not our initial aim, the methods employed might also offer insights to economists about the causality relation and timing of the response between consumer sentiment and stock price movements which are traditionally seen as being related through expectations about future consumer expenditure.

The rest of paper is organized as follows: in section 2, we provide background. We describe our method and experiments in section 3 and section 4 respectively. The conclusion and future works will be presented in section 5.

2 Background

In recent years many techniques have been applied to sentiment analysis for knowledge discovery in different domains. In early work on product recommendations (Turney, 2002) made use of an unsupervised learning approach to measure sentiment orientation for 410 Epinions reviews using adjectives and adverbs with respect to two anchor words, "excellent" and "poor". His method achieved an average 74% accuracy on four different review domains. (Pang et al., 2002) applied three supervised learners for classifying bidirectional sentiment in movie reviews, finding a number of challenges over traditional topic classification such as "thwarted expectations". (Hu and Liu, 2004) and (Dave et al., 2003) also performed product classification with the former focusing on the qualities of product features. (Mullen and Collier,

2004) used lexical clues from Epinion movie reviews and Pitchfork Media music reviews, yielding insights into the value of topical references.

With respect to identifying subjectivity, (Hatzivassiloglou and Wiebe, 2000)(Wiebe et al., 2001) examined the role of adjective classes for separating subjective from objective language.

The technologies used for determining sentiment orientation commonly include manual or semi-automatic methods for constructing sentiment lexicons, e.g. (Turney, 2002). (Das and Chen, 2007) in the stock analysis domain used a lexicon of finance words to help determine significant correlation between aggregated stock board messages by small investors and the Morgan Stanley High technology 35 Index (MSH35). However, they found the correlation was weak for individual stocks.

More recently, with the explosion of interest in social networks, a popular microblogging service called Twitter has become a major source for data-driven investigation. (Java et al., 2007)(Kwak et al., 2010) for example showed the social motivations of its users, and others (Zhao et al., 2007)(Lin et al., 2010)(Ritterman et al., 2009)(Petrović et al., 2010)(Petrovic et al., 2012) focused on breaking news or event detection. Sentiment analysis has been found to play an significant role in many applications (Krishnamurthy et al., 2008)(Bollen et al., 2011a)(Kivran-Swaine and Naaman, 2011) complementing evidence from Twitter messages and network structure.

In recent work on stock market prediction, (Bar-Haim et al., 2011) used Twitter messages (*Tweets*) from StockTwits to identify expert investors for predicting stock price rises. They used a support vector machine (SVM) to classify each stock related message to two polarities - "bullish" and "bearish" and then identified experts according to their success. The authors found that an unsupervised approach for identifying experts and combining their judgments achieved significantly higher precision than a random baseline, particularly for smaller numbers of experts. However, predictive performance was still low.(Bollen et al., 2011b) employed a set of expression patterns to extract opinions and then map those features into six sentiment orientations, "Calm", "Alert", "Sure", "Vital", "Kind" and "Happy" using a well-vetted psychometric instrument - the GPOMS (Google profit of mood state) algorithm. They trained a SOFNN (Self-Organizing Fuzzy Neural Network) and showed that one of the six mood dimensions called "Calm" was a statistically significant mood predictor for the DJIA daily price up and down change. However, (Bollen et al., 2011b)'s research only predicted movements in the DJIA index but it was not clear in which individual companies the user should invest.

3 Method

In this paper, we illustrate a hybrid method to train a series of classifiers for predicting the polarity of the daily market opening price change for four tech stocks namely Apple (AAPL), Google (GOOG), Microsoft (MSFT) and Amazon (AMZN). These were chosen because related topics such as their products, famous staff, etc. are all actively discussed in the social media. We also looked at other tech companies like Research In Motion Limited (RIMM), Yahoo (YHOO), etc. but found that the number of Tweets related to these companies is relatively small. Because we downloaded daily Tweets using the Twitter online streaming API called Firehose[1], we only had access to 1% of the Twitter corpus. Therefore, we expect the technique presented here to apply on a larger scale when we are able to access more of the Twitter corpus. Figure 1 shows an overview of the stock market prediction model.

[1]https://dev.twitter.com/docs/streaming-apis/streams/public

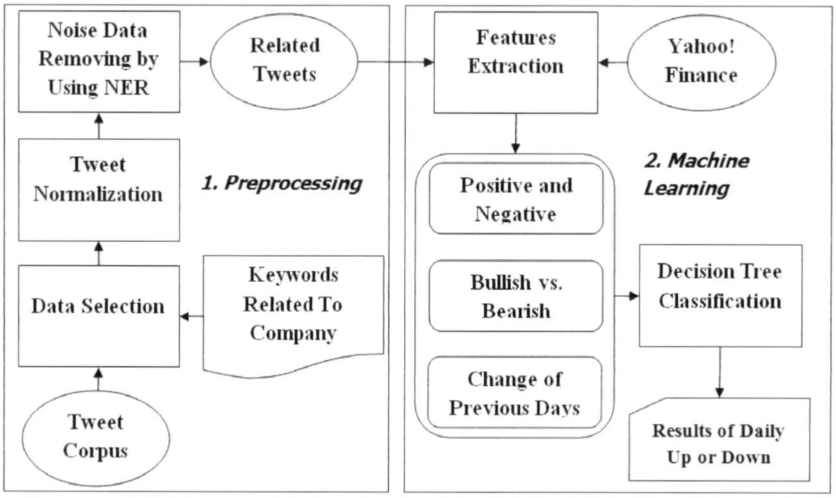

Figure 1: Daily up and down stock market prediction model

3.1 Data

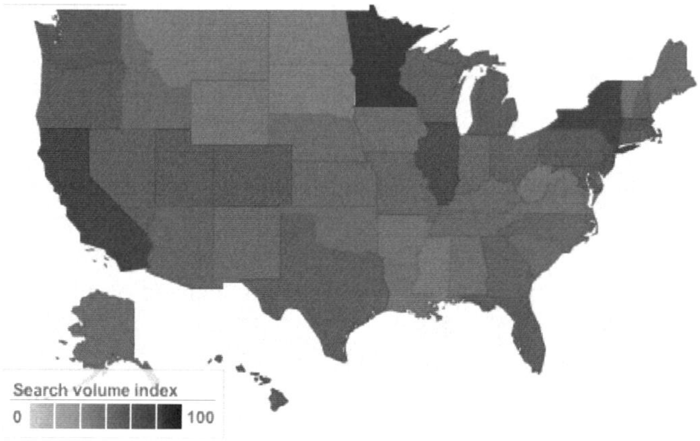

Figure 2: Keyword searching heat map (Apple).

Data containing 5,001,460 daily Tweets was crawled by using Twitter online streaming API from 1st April 2011 to 31st May 2011. In this initial investigation we would like to control the market sample to focus on the United States, so we geographically focused our Twitter queries on four large cities: New York, Chicago, Los Angeles and San Francisco. This also has some benefit in harmonising vocabulary – a recent study by (Gouws et al., 2011) noted significant differences in word abbreviation behaviour between British and American microtext authors. The Google Insights heat map[2] shown in figure 2 indicates that the people living in these four areas are more interested in the four companies. To compute the daily up and down of stock

[2]http://www.google.com/insights/search

market changes we employed Yahoo! Finance data using (1).

$$Move_i = OpenP_i - CloseP_{Pre(i)} = \begin{cases} \text{difference} >= 0 & \text{Raise} \\ \text{difference} < 0 & \text{Drop} \end{cases} \quad (1)$$

where i is a stock market open day, $Move_i$ is stock market change on day i, $OpenP_i$ is the opening price on day i, $CloseP_j$ is the closing price of a stock on day j and $Pre(i)$ is previous stock market open day of day i. In total we have 41 days of stock market open days of data excluding weekends and public holidays.

3.2 Time normalization

Before processing, we normalised the original Tweet time stamps to American Eastern Time, i.e. the NASDAQ stock market time, also taking into account changes in Winter time and Summer time. This data was then used to predict the following day's up or down movement in the four target stocks.

3.3 Preprocessing

3.3.1 Data selection

In this step, we aim to filter out those Tweets that are not relevant to the four target stocks. For the sake of simplicity this step introduces an assumption that the market as a whole (e.g. of mobile telephones) does not influence the stock price of an individual company. Starting from the names of the famous products of the four companies, we performed keyword more than factors we explore here expansion using Google Adwords[3] to create a list of terms for each stock. We filtered again to include only Tweets where users mention one of keywords. For example:

- AAPL: iphone, ipad, mac, ipod, ios, siri, apple store, itunes, etc.
- GOOG: google, gmail, gtalk, chrome, android, youtube, etc.
- MSFT: windows 7, windows 8, xbox, internet explorer, visual studio, office 2007, office 2010, etc.
- AMZN: alexa internet, amazon.com, amazon kindle, imdb, lovefilm, etc.

After keyword selection we can query for Tweets related to the companies.

3.3.2 Tweet normalization

When dealing with Tweets as has been reported in (Han and Baldwin, 2011), there is an issue of lexical normalization for out-of-vocabulary (OOV) words. Because around 15% of Tweets have 50% or more OOV tokens (Han and Baldwin, 2011), we applied the method proposed by (Han et al., 2012) to normalize Tweets. For example, with an input *"Ipad 2 is very cooooooooooooooollllllllllllllll"*

[3]https://adwords.google.com

- **First step:** each multiple character will be reduced to three. With the example, the output of this step is *"Ipad 2 is very cooolll"*
- **Second step:** apply normalization lexicon proposed by (Han et al., 2012) to normalize Tweets. For the example, the output of this step is *"Ipad 2 is very cool"*

We also normalized Tweet meta data, that is, every link becomes *LINK* and every account name becomes *ACCOUNT*. Hash tags are treated as normal words.

3.3.3 Noise data removing

After the normalization step, we wanted to identify Tweets on the topic of tech products, For example, although *"LOL YES !! RT : *ACCOUNT* : *ACCOUNT* You know we loved your Mac & Cheese Tweet. Can we turn it into a National television ad right now ?."* contains the *"mac"* keyword, it isn't a product of Apple corporation.

To resolve this problem, we built a Named Entity Recognition(NER) system to identify whether the Tweet contains name entities related to the companies or not based on a linear Conditional Random Fields(CRF) model. The Linear CRF model is used because it is well-studied and has been successfully used in state-of-the-art NER systems (Finkel et al., 2005)(Finkel and Manning, 2009)(Wang, 2009). If the Tweet doesn't contain any named entities as listed on the company keyword list, it is removed.

Twitter users are interested in named entities, such as, famous entrepreneurs, organization names, trendy hardware and software when they talk about tech companies. We collected and labelled manually 3665 randomly sampled Tweets related to the companies based on keywords. These included 280 people names (42 unique), 395 organization names (38 unique), 2528 hardware names (171 unique) and 1401 software names (294 unique). Overall, we have 4604 named entities in which 540 entities are unique.

Named entity recognition task

Given a Tweet as input, our task is to identify both the boundary and the class of each mention of entities of predefined types. We focus on four types of entities in our study, namely, persons, organizations, hardware, and software.

The following example illustrates our task. The input is "Only Apple can be surprising at not being surprising. I must be immune to the reality distortion field. Tell me when Lion & iOS 5 are out" The expected output is as follows:"Only <Organization>Apple</Organization> can be surprising at not being surprising. I must be immune to the reality distortion field. Tell me when <Software>Lion</Software> &; <Software>iOS 5</Software> are out", meaning that "Apple" is an organization, while "Lion" and "iOS 5" are software.

In our experiments, the CRF++[4] toolkit is used to train a linear CRF model. For each word, our CRF model extracts orthographic and lexical features based on (Wang, 2009) as follows:

- **Orthographic Features:** Word forms were mapped to a small number of standard orthographic classes. The present model uses 8 orthographic features to indicate whether the words are capitalised or upper case, whether they are alphanumeric or contain any slashes, whether the words are number or date, and whether the words are emails or punctuation marks.

[4]http://crfpp.sourceforge.net/

- **Lexical Features:** Every token in the training data was used as a feature. Alphabetic words in the training data were converted to lowercase, spelling errors detected in the proofreading stage were replaced by the correct resolution using the same technique in Tweet normalization step. Shorthand and abbreviations were expanded into bag of words (BOW) features. To utilise the context information, neighbouring words in the window [-2, +2] are also added as features $w_{i-2}, w_{i-1}, w_i, w_{i+1}, w_{i+2}$ where w_i is target word. A context window size of 2 is chosen because it yields the best performance.

After removing noise data, finally, the corpus for each company contained the following numbers of Tweets: AAPL (18,317), GOOG (28,435), AMZN (35,324), MSFT (4,023).

3.4 Machine Learning Framework

Following the main idea of behavioral finance theory (BFT) (Smith, 2003) and the efficient market hypothesis (EMH) (Fama, 1965), we make the assumption that the stock price can be predicted by using some features namely (1) sentiment related to the company: positive or negative, (2) the degree of market confidence: bullish or bearish. We then trained a Decision Tree(C4.5) classifier (Quinlan, 1993) by combining these features to address the text binary classification problem for predicting the daily up and down changes using our stock message set. Decision trees(Quinlan, 1993) have been widely used for prediction problems, often with good results (Cheung Chiu and Webb, 1998)(Wang and Chan, 2006).

Positive	:), :-), xd, (:, :p, :-p, ;), ;-), etc.
Negative	):, :(, :[, ;(, :{, ;'(, :'(, etc.

Table 1: Lexicon of emoticons

Positive	**Examples**
APPL	1. God I love my Iphone
	2. Yahoo!!! I finally bought the MacBook pro!!! :)
GOOG	3. Man, Google maps transit is awesome.
	4. Loving gmail motion and helvetica :)
MSFT	5. ...the Xbox & the Xbox 360 are the best designed consoles ever...
	6. hmm. i like this internet explorer 9
AMZN	7. Just saw this on Amazon: 'Kindle Wi-Fi' ... Cool:)
	8. got three books in the mail today. thank you amazon...
Negative	**Examples**
APPL	1. iPod battery low :(
	2. My iPhone no longer works on 3G networks... Boo :(
GOOG	3. my google chrome is being weird right now...:(
	4. New Google maps is very confused...
MSFT	5. Two things to never trust in Microsoft Word : spell check and grammar
	6. God hates me, and I hate Microsoft
AMZN	7. ...new sites that won't load due to the big Amazon AWS failure. :(
	8. Amazon servers went down, taking HootSuite and Foursquare down with it. :(

Table 2: Examples of positive/negative Tweets

3.4.1 Positive and Negative(Pos_Neg) features

To detect the sentiment of Tweets posted by Twitter users, we employ an online sentiment classifier called Twitter Sentiment Tool (TST)(Go et al., 2009). This tool is able to determine the polarity for a certain Tweet using a keyword-based algorithm. The polarity set contains three elements positive, neutral, negative. It is helpful to maximize the polarity distance between Tweets since we only need to be sure a query is positive or negative, and we ignore other Tweets (neutral). Furthermore, this online tool is ideally suited to our task since it is trained specifically on Twitter data. However, we still make a simple improvement before we send Tweets to TST. For example: *Caught up on the dvr. Time for bed. Must do laundry tomorrow, before I go and get my new ipad.:)*, this is obviously a positive sentiment for Apple but it is interesting that TST classifies this Tweet as Neutral. The designers (Go et al., 2009) of TST use emoticons as noisy labels to train the sentiment classifier so we expect this example to be Positive due to the ":)". Following from (Go et al., 2009)'s idea we created an emoticon lexicon shown in Table 1 to identify positive or negative of Tweets before we send Tweets to TST. Table 2 shows examples of positive/negative Tweets. After checking against the lexicon of emoticons in Table 1 and classifying with TST, we simply aggregate the number of positives and negatives for each day:

Positive feature is identified using (2,3).

$$PosDiff_i = \sum_{i} positive_i - \sum_{i-1} positive_{i-1} \tag{2}$$

$$Positive(D)_i = \begin{cases} 1 & \text{If } PosDiff_i >= 0 \\ 0 & \text{If } PosDiff_i < 0 \end{cases} \tag{3}$$

Where $positive_i$ denotes the number of positively classified message by TST for a particular company on day i. Similarly, the negative feature is identified by functions 4, 5.

$$NegDiff_i = \sum_{i} negative_i - \sum_{i-1} negative_{i-1} \tag{4}$$

$$Negative(D)_i = \begin{cases} 1 & \text{If } NegDiff_i >= 0 \\ 0 & \text{If } NegDiff_i < 0 \end{cases} \tag{5}$$

Where $negative_i$ denotes the number of negatively classified message by TST for a particular company on day i.

3.4.2 Bullish vs. Bearish features

To determine whether consumers have market confidence in the company, we made use of a Part-of-speech (POS) tagger to extract adjective, noun, adverb and verb words and fixed them to "bullish" and "bearish" as anchor words. We chose CMU POS Tagger proposed by (Gimpel et al., 2011) because this POS Tagger achieved the state of the art on Tweet data. We then calculated the anchor words using the Semantic Orientation (SO) algorithm (Turney, 2002). This algorithm uses mutual information to measure the association between two words. The

Pointwise Mutual Information (PMI) is formulated by function 6.

$$PMI(w_1, w_2) = \log_2\left(\frac{p(w_1\&w_2)}{p(w_1)p(w_2)}\right) \tag{6}$$

where w_1 and w_2 are two word strings. $p(w_1\&w_2)$ are the probability that both words co-occurred. $p(w_1)$ and $p(w_2)$ are the probability that an isolated word occurs. The ratio shows a metric of statistical dependence between w_1 and w_2. Thus, SO can be defined by (7).

$$SO(w) = PMI(w, \text{``}bullish'') - PMI(w, \text{``}bearish'') \tag{7}$$

Here, based on our anchor words, we redefined SO in (8).

$$SO(w) = \log_2\left(\frac{\#(wNEAR\text{``}bullish'')\#(\text{``}bearish'')}{\#(wNEAR\text{``}bearish'')\#(\text{``}bullish'')}\right) \tag{8}$$

To compute the equation 8, we used the AltaVista[5] search engine for the following reasons: (1) AltaVista only contains English webpages; (2) There is a location restriction that can allow us to focus on United States webpages, and (3) It provides a "NEAR" operator that helps to find documents containing pairs of words within 10 words distance of each other. (Turney, 2002) noted that the performance of the NEAR operator was better than the AND operator as a semantic association measure.

To avoid division by zero, we applied an add-one data smoothing method in queries whose result from AltaVista is zero, that is, a null hit. After this online training process, we build up a dictionary of four different POST: adjectives, nouns, adverbs, and verbs.

The bullish-bearish feature of Tweet day i is identified by functions 9, 10.

$$Bullish\_Bearish\_Diff_i = Bullish\_bearish_i - Bullish\_bearish_{i-1} \tag{9}$$

$$Bullish\_Bearish(D)_i = \begin{cases} 1 & \text{If } Bullish\_Bearish\_Diff_i >= 0 \\ 0 & \text{If } Bullish\_Bearish\_Diff_i < 0 \end{cases} \tag{10}$$

Where $Bullish\_Bearish_i$ denotes the mean of SO values of all extracted words in day i.

3.4.3 Stock market changes on price previous days

To predict stock market movement on day i, we applied in previous days $(i-1, i-2, i-3, ...)$as features to train the classifier. Number of previous days is experimentally identified as 3 to yield the highest performance.

Finally, the changes of three previous days were combined with the previous fixed features - positive, negative and bullish/bearish to get the best performance calculated by the Decision Tree classifier(Quinlan, 1993).

[5]http://www.altavista.com/

4 Experimental Results

4.1 Main results

Due to the limited corpus size of 41 days in the training set, and also considering the over-fitting problem, we chose the 10-fold cross validation method to estimate the accuracy of our approach. We trained our classifier using Decision Tree (C4.5) with features generated from previous day data. This is because our analysis shown in Table 3 indicates that Pos_Neg features have the lowest p-value in the Granger-Causality Test with 1 day lag. Granger causality analysis rests on the assumption that if a variable X causes Y then changes in X will systematically occur before changes in Y . We will thus find that the lagged values of X will exhibit a statistically significant correlation with Y . Correlation however does not prove causation. We therefore use Granger causality analysis in a similar fashion to (Gilbert and Karahalios, 2010); we are not testing actual causation but whether one time series has predictive information about the other or not. All methods used filtering with NER. Table 4 shows daily prediction accuracy on Apple Inc., Google, Amazon, and Microsoft stock prices respectively.

Lag	AAPL		GOOG		MSFT		AMZN	
	PF	NF	PF	NF	PF	NF	PF	NF
1 day	**0.004****	0.144	0.107	**0.018***	0.539	**0.34**	**0.032***	0.76
2 days	**0.012***	0.24	0.4	0.12	0.96	0.81	0.11	0.83
3 days	0.051	0.44	0.265	0.072	0.865	0.879	0.074	0.749
4 days	0.056	0.589	0.587	0.289	0.924	0.984	0.156	0.829
5 days	0.102	0.326	0.241	0.143	0.975	0.713	0.443	0.877
6 days	0.1	0.361	0.095	0.156	0.981	0.775	0.282	0.576
7 days	0.27	0.47	0.119	0.3	0.903	0.781	0.406	0.63

Table 3: Statistical significance (P-Values) of Granger-Causality Test between Pos_Neg features and stock market movement of four companies in period April 1, 2011 to May 31, 2011. ***PF:* Positive Feature, *NF:* Negative Feature (p-value $<$ 0.01: **, p-value $<$ 0.05: *)**

Method	AAPL	GOOG	MSFT	AMZN
Only bullish/bearish	53.66%	58.54%	56.10%	37.50%
Only previous days	51.22%	53.66%	73.73%	37.50%
Only Pos_Neg	73.17%	68.29%	56.10%	71.88%
Bullish/bearish + previous days	63.41%	63.41%	**75.61%**	62.50%
Bullish/bearish + Pos_Neg	73.17%	70.73%	56.10%	71.88%
Pos_Neg + previous days	73.17%	68.29%	70.73%	71.88%
Pos_Neg + bullish/bearish + previous days	**82.93%**	**80.49%**	**75.61%**	**75.00%**

Table 4: Prediction accuracy on each stock

The results shown in Table 4 indicate a surprisingly high level of accuracy for stock price polarity prediction using our proposed model. The combination of all Pos_Neg, bullish/bearish, and previous change yields superior performance for all stocks.

No single feature obviously stands out as superior in all Apple, Google, Microsoft and Amazon stocks. Pos_Neg features can predict well for Apple, Google, Amazon with accuracies of 73.17%, 68.29%, and 71.88% but result is a fall for Microsoft with accuracy of only 56.10%. The accuracies consistent to Granger Causality Test's results shown in Table 3 that we can reject

NULL hypothesis that the mood time series does not predict APPL, GOOG, and AMZN stock markets (P-value < 0.05). Pos_Neg features cannot predict well Microsoft stock because the number of Pos_Neg Tweets is very few (over 20 days have no Pos_Neg Tweets). So in the case of frequent Pos_Neg Tweets, Pos_Neg features appear to function as a strong prediction of stock market movement.

The previous day's price movement and Bullish/bearish features seem to offer explicitly weaker predictability. However when we combine these two features, the predictability of our system improves significantly, for example, from 37.50% to 62.50% on Amazon stock. The other combination of two features can slightly increase our system's predictability, for example, the combination of Pos_Neg and Bullish/bearish features made an improvement of Google's accuracy from 68.29% to 70.73%.

The combination of Previous days's price movement, Bullish/bearish and Pos_Neg features create a superior model in all Apple, Google, Microsoft and Amazon stocks. Accuracies for our stock market prediction system increase to a peak of 82.93%, 80.49%, 75.61% and 75.00% in Apple, Google, Microsoft and Amazon respectively.

To show the effectiveness and correctness of the proposed model, we applied the model with a combination of Previous days's price movement, Bullish/bearish and Pos_Neg features to an online test in which we accessed realtime Tweets using the Twitter online streaming API. The online test was implemented from 8th September 2012 to 26th September 2012. Table 5 shows the experimental results of the online test with high prediction accuracies of 76.92%, 76.92%, 69.23% and 84.62% in Apple, Google, Microsoft and Amazon respectively. The online experimental result provides an additional indication of the effectiveness and correctness of our proposed model.

Stock market	Accuracy
AAPL	76.92%
GOOG	76.92%
MSFT	69.23%
AMZN	84.62%

Table 5: Experimental results in the online test

We note that the results offer a company analysis level in contrast with (Bollen et al., 2011b)'s research. Although (Bollen et al., 2011b) achieved accuracy of 87.6% in predicting the daily up and down changes in the closing values of the Dow Jones industrial average, it was not clear which companies the user should invest in. Again, in contrast to (Bollen et al., 2011b), we do not need specialized sentiment lexicons. Although the result is not directly comparable with (Bar-Haim et al., 2011), because of differences in the size of the data set and the number of stocks studied, it provides *prima facie* evidence for a much higher level of predictive performance using sentiment related to company specific features over identification of expert stock pickers. The result also indicates that company related sentiment can offer strong correlation to individual stock prices in contrast to (Das and Chen, 2007)'s experience with stock board messages. The number of days and the number of stocks in our experiment should make us cautious about making strong conclusion from the results. Nevertheless we believe the result are indicative of interesting trends that should be followed up in future works.

Entity Type	Precision	Recall	F-score
Hardware	97.06%	84.33%	90.24%
Software	94.78%	70.78%	81.02%
Organization	92.82%	66.51%	77.03%
Person	100%	81.12%	89.20%
All Entities	**90.02%**	**78.08%**	**83.60%**

Table 6: Overall NER experimental results

Stock market	Accuracy with NER	Accuracy without NER
AAPL	**82.93%**	73.17%
GOOG	**80.49%**	75.61%
MSFT	**75.61%**	68.29%
AMZN	**75.00%**	71.88%

Table 7: Effectiveness of Using Named Entity Recognition in tech stock market prediction by all using Pos_Neg, bullish/bearish and previous days features

4.2 NER experimental results

We randomly selected 3665 Tweets related to the companies using keywords. After that, the Tweets were labeled manually by one of the authors, so that the beginning and the end of each named entity is marked as <TYPE> and </TYPE>, respectively. This then formed the gold-standard data set. Here TYPE is SOFTWARE, HARDWARE, ORGANIZATION, or PERSON. The gold-standard data set is evenly split into ten parts to implement ten folds test: nine for training and one for testing. We use Precision, Recall, and F-score as the evaluation metrics. Precision is a measure of the percentage of correct output labels, and recall tells us the percentage correctly labelled in the gold-standard data set, while F1 is the harmonic mean of precision and recall. The NER experimental results are showed in Table 6.

The overall NER experimental result is good with Precision of 90.02%, Recall of 78.08%, and F-score of 83.60%. We can achieve high performance in the NER system for the following reasons. Firstly, although 3665 Tweets were used as the golden corpus to train and test the NER system, there are 280 people names (42 unique), 395 organization names (38 unique), 2528 hardware names (171 unique) and 1401 software names (294 unique). Overall, we have 4604 named entities in which 540 entities are unique. So it made the training set cover most contexts of these entities. Secondly, the Tweet's informal nature causes the low performance of recent NER systems on Tweet data (Liu et al., 2011). To overtake that problem, we use normalization technique (Han and Baldwin, 2011) on Tweet data before applying the NER system, leading to the high performance.

4.3 Effects of NER to remove noise

Table 7 shows the performance of the best performing method in Table 4 (Pos_Neg + bullish/bearish + previous days) with and without using NER system to remove noise. NER filter step plays a very important role in our system. Without this step, the performance of our system decreases significantly to 73.17%, 75.61%, 68.29%, and 71.88% for all stocks. We further check the data before and after the noise-removal step. There were many unrelated Pos_Neg Tweets removed for all companies. It helps the identification of positive and negative features by functions 2,3,4,5 and bullish vs bearish feature by functions 6,7,8 to be more accurate.

5 Conclusion and Future Work

In this paper we have addressed the problem of predicting daily up and down movements in individual tech stock prices using a combination of three feature types from Twitter messages related to the company: positive and negative sentiment, consumer confidence in the product with respect to bullish and bearish lexicon, and the change on three previous days of stock market price. The features were employed in a Decision Tree(C4.5) classifier to yield high levels of accuracies of 82.93%,80.49%, 75.61% and 75.00% in predicting the daily up and down changes of Apple (AAPL), Google (GOOG), Microsoft (MSFT) and Amazon (AMZN) stocks respectively. We also indicated the influence of each features to the results of our proposed model. Especially, the experimental results showed that using NER to remove noise data played a very important role in the stock market prediction model.

The study we have presented has been limited to 41 days of Tweets so we must regard any results as indicative rather than conclusive. In future work, with access to more data, we would like to expand our investigation to a longer time frame and a wider range of companies as well as looking at shorter market durations.

Acknowledgments

This work was done when the first author was an internship student in the National Institute of Informatics(NII), Tokyo, Japan. And this work was supported by NII. We thank the reviewers for their valuable comments.

References

Bar-Haim, R., Dinur, E., Feldman, R., Fresko, M., and Goldstein, G. (2011). Identifying and following expert investors in stock microblogs. In *Proceedings of the Conference on Empirical Methods in Natural Language Processing*, EMNLP '11, pages 1310–1319, Stroudsburg, PA, USA. Association for Computational Linguistics.

Bollen, J., Gonçalves, B., Ruan, G., and Mao, H. (2011a). Happiness is assortative in online social networks. *CoRR*, abs/1103.0784.

Bollen, J., Mao, H., and Zeng, X. (2011b). Twitter mood predicts the stock market. *Journal of Computational Science*, 2(1):1 – 8.

Cheung Chiu, B. and Webb, G. I. (1998). Using decision trees for agent modeling: Improving prediction performance. *User Modeling and User-Adapted Interaction*, 8(1-2):131–152.

Das, S. R. and Chen, M. Y. (2007). Yahoo! for Amazon: Sentiment extraction from small talk on the Web. volume 53, pages 1375–1388.

Dave, K., Lawrence, S., and Pennock, D. M. (2003). Mining the peanut gallery: opinion extraction and semantic classification of product reviews. In *Proceedings of the 12th international conference on World Wide Web*, WWW '03, pages 519–528, New York, NY, USA. ACM.

Fama, E. F. (1965). The Behavior of Stock-Market Prices. *The Journal of Business*, 38(1):34–105.

Finkel, J. R., Grenager, T., and Manning, C. (2005). Incorporating non-local information into information extraction systems by gibbs sampling. In *Proceedings of the 43rd Annual Meeting on Association for Computational Linguistics*, ACL '05, pages 363–370, Stroudsburg, PA, USA. Association for Computational Linguistics.

Finkel, J. R. and Manning, C. D. (2009). Nested named entity recognition. In *Proceedings of the 2009 Conference on Empirical Methods in Natural Language Processing: Volume 1 - Volume 1*, EMNLP '09, pages 141–150, Stroudsburg, PA, USA. Association for Computational Linguistics.

Gilbert, E. and Karahalios, K. (2010). Widespread worry and the stock market. In *In Proceedings of the International Conference on Weblogs and Social*.

Gimpel, K., Schneider, N., O'Connor, B., Das, D., Mills, D., Eisenstein, J., Heilman, M., Yogatama, D., Flanigan, J., and Smith, N. A. (2011). Part-of-speech tagging for twitter: annotation, features, and experiments. In *Proceedings of the 49th Annual Meeting of the Association for Computational Linguistics: Human Language Technologies: short papers - Volume 2*, HLT '11, pages 42–47, Stroudsburg, PA, USA. Association for Computational Linguistics.

Go, A., Bhayani, R., and Huang, L. (2009). Twitter sentiment classification using distant supervision. Technical report, Stanford University.

Gouws, S., Metzler, D., Cai, C., and Hovy, E. (2011). Contextual bearing on linguistic variation in social media. In *Proceedings of the Workshop on Languages in Social Media*, LSM '11, pages 20–29, Stroudsburg, PA, USA. Association for Computational Linguistics.

Han, B. and Baldwin, T. (2011). Lexical normalisation of short text messages: makn sens a #twitter. In *Proceedings of the 49th Annual Meeting of the Association for Computational Linguistics: Human Language Technologies - Volume 1*, HLT '11, pages 368–378, Stroudsburg, PA, USA. Association for Computational Linguistics.

Han, B., Cook, P., and Baldwin, T. (2012). Automatically constructing a normalisation dictionary for microblogs. In *Proceedings of the 2012 Joint Conference on Empirical Methods in Natural Language Processing and Computational Natural Language Learning (EMNLP-CoNLL 2012)*, pages 421–432, Jeju Island, Korea.

Hatzivassiloglou, V. and Wiebe, J. M. (2000). Effects of adjective orientation and gradability on sentence subjectivity. In *Proceedings of the 18th conference on Computational linguistics - Volume 1*, COLING '00, pages 299–305, Stroudsburg, PA, USA. Association for Computational Linguistics.

Hu, M. and Liu, B. (2004). Mining and summarizing customer reviews. In *Proceedings of the tenth ACM SIGKDD international conference on Knowledge discovery and data mining*, KDD '04, pages 168–177, New York, NY, USA. ACM.

Java, A., Song, X., Finin, T., and Tseng, B. (2007). Why we twitter: understanding microblogging usage and communities. In *Proceedings of the 9th WebKDD and 1st SNA-KDD 2007 workshop on Web mining and social network analysis*, WebKDD/SNA-KDD '07, pages 56–65, New York, NY, USA. ACM.

Kivran-Swaine, F. and Naaman, M. (2011). Network properties and social sharing of emotions in social awareness streams. In *Proceedings of the ACM 2011 conference on Computer supported cooperative work*, CSCW '11, pages 379–382, New York, NY, USA. ACM.

Krishnamurthy, B., Gill, P., and Arlitt, M. (2008). A few chirps about twitter. In *Proceedings of the first workshop on Online social networks*, WOSN '08, pages 19–24, New York, NY, USA. ACM.

Kwak, H., Lee, C., Park, H., and Moon, S. (2010). What is twitter, a social network or a news media? In *Proceedings of the 19th international conference on World wide web*, WWW '10, pages 591–600, New York, NY, USA. ACM.

Lin, C. X., Zhao, B., Mei, Q., and Han, J. (2010). Pet: a statistical model for popular events tracking in social communities. In *Proceedings of the 16th ACM SIGKDD international conference on Knowledge discovery and data mining*, KDD '10, pages 929–938, New York, NY, USA. ACM.

Liu, X., Zhang, S., Wei, F., and Zhou, M. (2011). Recognizing named entities in tweets. In *Proceedings of the 49th Annual Meeting of the Association for Computational Linguistics: Human Language Technologies - Volume 1*, HLT '11, pages 359–367, Stroudsburg, PA, USA. Association for Computational Linguistics.

Mullen, T. and Collier, N. (2004). Sentiment analysis using support vector machines with diverse information sources. In *In Proceedings of Conference on Empirical Methods in Natural Language Processing*, pages 412–418.

Pang, B., Lee, L., and Vaithyanathan, S. (2002). Thumbs up?: sentiment classification using machine learning techniques. In *Proceedings of the ACL-02 conference on Empirical methods in natural language processing - Volume 10*, EMNLP '02, pages 79–86, Stroudsburg, PA, USA. Association for Computational Linguistics.

Petrović, S., Osborne, M., and Lavrenko, V. (2010). Streaming first story detection with application to twitter. In *Human Language Technologies: The 2010 Annual Conference of the North American Chapter of the Association for Computational Linguistics*, HLT '10, pages 181–189, Stroudsburg, PA, USA. Association for Computational Linguistics.

Petrovic, S., Osborne, M., and Lavrenko, V. (2012). Using paraphrases for improving first story detection in news and twitter. In *HLT-NAACL*, pages 338–346.

Quinlan, J. R. (1993). *C4.5: programs for machine learning*. Morgan Kaufmann Publishers Inc., San Francisco, CA, USA.

Ritterman, J., Osborne, M., and Klein, E. (2009). Using prediction markets and Twitter to predict a swine flu pandemic. In *Proceedings of the 1st International Workshop on Mining Social Media*.

Smith, V. L. (2003). Constructivist and ecological rationality in economics. pages 502–561.

Turney, P. D. (2002). Thumbs up or thumbs down?: semantic orientation applied to unsupervised classification of reviews. In *Proceedings of the 40th Annual Meeting on Association for Computational Linguistics*, ACL '02, pages 417–424, Stroudsburg, PA, USA. Association for Computational Linguistics.

Wang, J.-L. and Chan, S.-H. (2006). Stock market trading rule discovery using two-layer bias decision tree. *Expert Syst. Appl.*, 30(4):605–611.

Wang, Y. (2009). Annotating and recognising named entities in clinical notes. In *Proceedings of the ACL-IJCNLP 2009 Student Research Workshop*, pages 18–26, Suntec, Singapore. Association for Computational Linguistics.

Wiebe, J., Bruce, R., Bell, M., Martin, M., and Wilson, T. (2001). A corpus study of evaluative and speculative language. In *Proceedings of the Second SIGdial Workshop on Discourse and Dialogue - Volume 16*, SIGDIAL '01, pages 1–10, Stroudsburg, PA, USA. Association for Computational Linguistics.

Zhao, Q., Mitra, P., and Chen, B. (2007). Temporal and information flow based event detection from social text streams. In *Proceedings of the 22nd national conference on Artificial intelligence - Volume 2*, AAAI'07, pages 1501–1506. AAAI Press.

End-to-End Sentiment Analysis of Twitter Data

Apoorv Agarwal[1] *Jasneet Singh Sabharwal*[2]
(1) Columbia University, NY, U.S.A.
(2) Guru Gobind Singh Indraprastha University, New Delhi, India
apoorv@cs.columbia.edu, jasneet.sabharwal@gmail.com

Abstract
In this paper, we present an end-to-end pipeline for sentiment analysis of a popular micro-blogging website called Twitter. We acknowledge that much of current research adheres to parts of this pipeline. However, to the best of our knowledge, there is no work that explores the classifier design issues explored in this paper. We build a hierarchal cascaded pipeline of three models to label a tweet as one of Objective, Neutral, Positive, Negative class. We compare the performance of this hierarchal pipeline with that of a 4-way classification scheme. In addition, we explore the trade-off between making a prediction on lesser number of tweets versus F1-measure. Overall we show that a cascaded design is better than a 4-way classifier design.

Keywords: Sentiment analysis, Twitter, cascaded model design, classifier confidence.

1 Introduction

Microblogging websites have evolved to become a source of varied kind of information. This is due to nature of microblogs on which people post real time messages about their opinions on a variety of topics, discuss current issues, complain, and express positive sentiment for products they use in daily life. In fact, companies manufacturing such products have started to poll these microblogs to get a sense of general sentiment for their product. Many times these companies study user reactions and reply to users on microblogs.[1] One challenge is to build technology to detect and summarize an overall sentiment.

In this paper, we look at one such popular micro-blog called Twitter[2] and propose an end-to-end pipeline for classifying tweets into one of four categories: *Objective, Neutral, Positive, Negative*. Traditionally, *Objective* category is defined as text segments containing facts and devoid of opinion (Pang and Lee, 2004; Wilson et al., 2005). In the context of micro-blogs, we extend this definition to include intelligible text, like "SAPSPKSAPKOASKOP SECAFLOZ PSOKASPKOA". Note, since we are only concerned with sentiment analysis of English language micro-blogs, text in other languages will also fall under the intelligible category and thus under Objective text.

One option to classify tweets into one of the four aforementioned categories is to simply implement a 4-way classifier. Another option is to build a cascaded design, stacking 3 classifiers on top of each other: Objective versus Subjective, Polar versus Non-polar and Positive versus Negative. In this paper, we explore these possibilities of building a classifier. In addition, we study the trade-off between making predictions on lesser number of examples versus F1-measure. If the confidence of the classifier falls below a threshold, we reserve prediction on that example. In expectation, this will boost the F1-measure, because we are reserving prediction on *harder* examples. But a-priori the

[1] http://mashable.com/2010/04/19/sentiment-analysis/
[2] www.twitter.com

Proceedings of the Workshop on Information Extraction and Entity Analytics on Social Media Data, pages 29–34,
COLING 2012, Mumbai, December 2012.

relation between the two (threshold and F1-measure) is unclear. Moreover, it is unclear in which of the aforementioned three designs, this trade-off is least. We present this relation graphically and show that one of the cascaded designs is significantly better than the other designs.

We use manually annotated Twitter data for our experiments. Part of the data, Positive, Negative and Neutral labeled tweets were introduced and made publicly available in (Agarwal et al., 2011). Annotations for tweets belonging to the *Objective* category are made publicly available through this work.[3]

In this paper, we do not introduce a new feature space or explore new machine learning paradigms for classification. For feature design and exploration of the best machine learning model, we use our previous work (Agarwal et al., 2011).

2 Literature Survey

In most of the traditional literature on sentiment analysis, researchers have addressed the binary task of separating text into Positive and Negative categories (Turney, 2002; Hu and Liu, 2004; Kim and Hovy, 2004). However, there is early work on building classifiers for first detecting if a text is Subjective or Objective followed by separating Subjective text into Positive and Negative classes (Pang and Lee, 2004). The definition of Subjective class for Pang and Lee (2004) contains only Positive and Negative classes, in contrast to more recent work of Wilson et al. (2005), who additionally consider Neutral class to be part of Subjective class. Yu and Hatzivassiloglou (2003) build classifiers for the binary task Subjective versus Objective and the ternary task Neutral, Positive and Negative. However, they do not explore the 4-way design or the cascaded design. One of the earliest work to explore these design issues is by Wilson et al. (2005). They compare a 3-way classifier that separates news snippets into one of three categories: Neutral, Positive and Negative, to a cascaded design of two classifiers: Polar versus Non-polar and Positive versus Negative. They defined Polar to contain both Positive and Negative class and Non-polar to contain only Neutral class. We extend on their work to compare a 4-way classifier to a cascaded design of three models: Objective versus Subjective, Polar versus Non-polar and Positive versus Negative. Note, this extension poses a question about training the Polar versus Non-polar model: should Non-polar category only contain Neutral examples or both Neutral and Objective. Of course, the 4-way classifier puts all three categories (Objective, Positive and Negative) together while training a model to detect Neutral. In this paper, we explore these designs.

In the context of micro-blogs such as Twitter, to the best of our knowledge, we know of no literature that explores this issue. Barbosa and Feng (2010) build two separate classifiers, one for Subjective versus Objective classes and one for Positive versus Negative classes. They present separate evaluation on both models but do not explore combining them or comparing it with a 3-way classification scheme. More recently, (Jiang et al., 2011) present results on building a 3-way classifier for Objective, Positive and Negative tweets. However, they do not explore the cascaded design and do not detect Neutral tweets. Moreover, to the best of our knowledge, there is no work in the literature that studies the trade-off between making less predictions and F1-measure. Like human annotations, predictions made by machines have confidence levels. In this paper, we compare the 3 classifier designs in terms of their ability to predict better given a chance to make predictions only on examples they are most confident on.

[3]Due to Twitter's recent policy, we might only be able to provide the tweet identifiers and their annotation publicly available: http://www.readwriteweb.com/archives/how_recent_changes_to_twitters_terms_of_service_mi.php

3 End-to-end pipeline with cascaded Models

The pipeline for end-to-end classification of tweets into one of four categories is simple: 1) crawl the tweets from the web, 2) pre-process and normalize the tweets, 3) extract features and finally 4) build classifiers that classify the tweets into one of four categories: Objective, Neutral, Positive, Negative.

We use our previous work for pre-processing, feature extraction and selection of suitable classifier (Agarwal et al., 2011). We found Support Vector Machines (SVMs) to perform the best and therefore all our models in this paper are supervised SVM models using *Senti-features* from our previous work.

The main contribution of this work is the exploration of classifier designs. Following is a list of possible classifier designs:

1. Build a **4-way** classifier. Note, in a 4-way classification scheme, a multi-class one-versus-all SVM builds 4 models, one for identifying each class. Each model is built by treating one class as positive and the remaining three classes as negative. Given an unseen example, the classifier passes this through the four models and predicts the class with highest confidence (as given by the four models).

2. Build a hierarchy of 3 cascaded models: Objective versus Subjective, Polar versus Non-Polar and Positive versus Negative. But there is one design decision to be taken here: while building the Polar versus Non-polar model, do we want to treat both Neutral and Objective examples as Non-polar or only Neutral examples as Non-polar? This decision affects the way we create the Polar versus Non-polar model. Note, a 4-way model, implicitly treats Neutral to be Non-polar and the remaining three classes to be Polar. This scenario is unsatisfying because a-priori there is no reason why Objective examples should be treated as Polar at the time of training. We explore both these options:

   (a) **PNP-neutral**: Polar versus Non-polar model, where only Neutral examples are treated as Non-polar whereas Positive and Negative examples combined are treated as Polar.

   (b) **PNP-objective-neutral**: Polar versus Non-polar model, where Neutral and Objective examples combined are treated as Non-polar whereas Positive and Negative examples combined are treated as Polar.

In this paper, we present results for each of the aforementioned design decisions in training models. Moreover, we explore the trade-off between predicting on fewer number of examples and its affect on the F1-measure. It is not hard to imagine, especially when the output of the classifier is presented to humans for judgement, that we might want to reserve predictions on examples where the classifier confidence is low. A recent example scenario is that of Watson (Ferrucci et al., 2010) playing the popular gameshow Jeopardy! Watson buzzed in to answer a question only if it was confident over a certain threshold. We perform classification with **filtering**, i.e. considering classifier confidence along with its prediction. If the classifier confidence is below a certain threshold, we do not make a prediction on such examples. If for some value of threshold, θ, we reserve predictions on say x test examples, and say the total number of test examples is N, then the **Rejection rate** is given by $\frac{x}{N} * 100\%$.

Class	# instances for training	# instances for testing
Objective	1859	629
Neutral	1029	344
Positive	1042	350
Negative	1020	327

Table 1: Number of instances of each class used for training and testing

4 Experiments and Results

In this section, we present experiments and results for each of the pipelines described in section 3: 4-way, PNP-only-neutral and PNP-objective-neutral.

Experimental Setup: For all our experiments, we use support vector machines with linear classifier to create the models. We perform cross-validation to choose the right C value that determines the cost of mis-classifying an example at the time of learning. We report results on an unseen test set whose distribution is given in Table 1.

4.1 Classifier design

As explained in section 3, it is not clear a-priori, which of the three design decisions (4-way, PNP-neutral, PNP-objective-neutral) is most appropriate for building and end-to-end pipeline for sentiment analysis of Twitter data. Our results show that that PNP-objective-neutral gives a statistically significantly higher F1-measure for Neutral category, while giving same ball-park F1-measure for other three categories as compared to the other two design options.

	4-way			PNP-neutral			PNP-objective-neutral		
Category	P	R	F1	P	R	F1	P	R	F1
Objective	0.70	0.87	**0.78**	0.77	0.76	0.76	0.78	0.76	0.77
Neutral	0.51	0.30	0.38	0.48	0.22	0.31	0.39	0.46	**0.42**
Negative	0.56	0.56	0.56	0.49	0.64	0.56	0.57	0.57	**0.57**
Positive	0.59	0.56	0.57	0.51	0.67	**0.58**	0.61	0.53	0.57
Average	0.59	0.57	0.57	0.56	0.57	0.55	0.59	0.58	**0.58**

Table 2: Results for different classifier designs as mentioned in section 3. Note all numbers are rounded off to 2 significant digits.

Table 2 presents the result for the three design choices. For predicting the Objective class, all three designs perform in the same ball-park. For predicting the Neutral class, PNP-objective-neutral is significantly better than 4-way and PNP-neutral, achieving an F1-measure of 0.42 as compared to 0.38 and 0.31 respectively. For predicting the remaining two classes, Positive and Negative, the performance of the three designs is in the same ball-park.

4.2 Trade-off between Rejection rate versus F1-measure

Figure 1 presents a plot of rejection rate (on x-axis) versus mean F1-measure (on y-axis) for 4-way design (dotted green curve) and for PNP-objective-neutral (solid blue curve). The plot for the third design (PNP-neutral) is in the middle of these two curves and is omitted for clarity.

First thing to note is that the rejection rate always increases faster than in F1-measure.

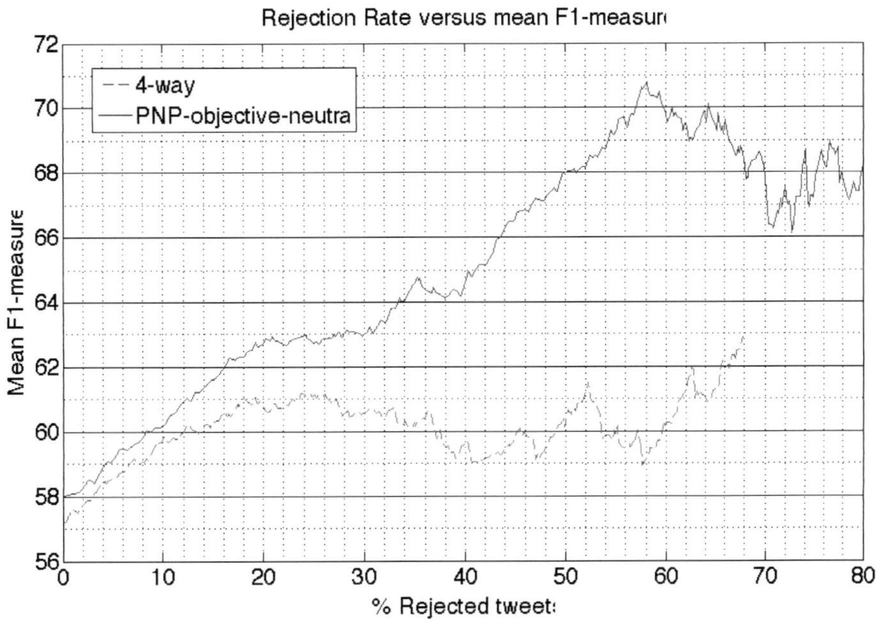

Figure 1: Rejection rate (on x-axis) versus mean F1-measure (on y-axis) for 4-way design (dotted green curve) and for PNP-objective-neutral (solid blue curve).

$$P = \frac{tp}{tp+fp}; R = \frac{tp}{tp+fn}; F1 = \frac{2PR}{P+R} = \frac{tp}{2tp+fp+fn}$$

where, P is precision, R is recall, $F1$ is F1-measure, tp is number of true positive, fn is number of false negative, and fp is number of false positive.

In the best case scenario, reserving predictions will lead to decrease in number of false positives and false negatives, without affecting true positives. So as x (number of test examples on which we reserve predictions) increases, rejection rate increases, and $fp + fn$ decreases (all linearly). Therefore, $F1 \propto \frac{1}{2+\frac{1}{x}} = \frac{x}{2x+1}$. It is easy to check that x grows faster than $F1$.

Second, the increase in the mean F-measure for PNP-objective-neutral grows at a higher rate as compared to the 4-way classifier. What this translates to is that the 4-way classifier is classifying true positives with lower confidence as compared to the cascaded model design, PNP-objective-neutral. Differently put, PNP-objective-neutral is eliminating more false positive and false negatives, which it is not confident about, as compared to 4-way. Comparing the maximum mean F-measure achieved by both designs, we see that 4-way achieves the mean maximum F-measure of 0.63 at a rejection rate of 67.81% as compare to PNP-objective-neutral, which achieves a higher maximum mean F-measure of 0.71 at a lower rejection rate of 58.12%.

Conclusion and Future Work

We conclude that overall PNP-objective-neutral is a better design. In the future we would like to study the nature of examples that the classifier deems *hard* and its correlation with what humans think is *hard*. For this we will need human confidence on their annotations.

References

Agarwal, A., Xie, B., Vovsha, I., Rambow, O., and Passonneau, R. (2011). Sentiment analysis of twitter data. In *Proceedings of the Workshop on Language in Social Media (LSM 2011)*, pages 30–38, Portland, Oregon. Association for Computational Linguistics.

Barbosa, L. and Feng, J. (2010). Robust sentiment detection on twitter from biased and noisy data. *Proceedings of the 23rd International Conference on Computational Linguistics: Posters*, pages 36–44.

Ferrucci, D. A., Brown, E. W., Chu-Carroll, J., Fan, J., Gondek, D., Kalyanpur, A., Lally, A., Murdock, J. W., Nyberg, E., Prager, J. M., Schlaefer, N., and Welty, C. A. (2010). Building watson: An overview of the deepqa project. *AI Magazine*, 31:59–79.

Go, A., Bhayani, R., and Huang, L. (2009). Twitter sentiment classification using distant supervision. Technical report, Stanford.

Hu, M. and Liu, B. (2004). Mining and summarizing customer reviews. *KDD*.

Jiang, L., Yu, M., Zhou, M., Liu, X., and Zhao, T. (2011). Target-dependent twitter sentiment classification. *49th Annual Meeting of Association of Computational Linguistics*, pages 151–160.

Kim, S. M. and Hovy, E. (2004). Determining the sentiment of opinions. *Coling*.

Pak, A. and Paroubek, P. (2010). Twitter as a corpus for sentiment analysis and opinion mining. *Proceedings of LREC*.

Pang, B. and Lee, L. (2004). A sentimental education: Sentiment analysis using subjectivity analysis using subjectivity summarization based on minimum cuts. *ACL*.

Turney, P. (2002). Thumbs up or thumbs down? seman- tic orientation applied to unsupervised classification of reviews. *ACL*.

Whissel, C. M. (1989). *The dictionary of Affect in Language*. Emotion: theory research and experience, Acad press London.

Wilson, T., Wiebe, J., and Hoffman, P. (2005). Recognizing contextual polarity in phrase level sentiment analysis. *ACL*.

Wu, Y., Zhang, Q., Huang, X., and Wu, L. (2009). Phrase dependency parsing for opinion mining. In *Proceedings of the 2009 Conference on Empirical Methods in Natural Language Processing*, pages 1533–1541, Singapore. Association for Computational Linguistics.

Yu, H. and Hatzivassiloglou, V. (2003). Towards answering opinion questions: Separating facts from opinions and identifying the polarity of opinion sentences. *Conference on Empirical methods in natural language processing*, 10:129–136.

Author Index